WORLD CHRISTIANITY

southern africa

A factual portrait
of the Christian Church
in South Africa, Botswana,
Lesotho, Namibia
and Swaziland

❁

MARJORIE FROISE, Editor
Edward R. Dayton, Series Editor

LCWE

MARC

MARC (Missions Advanced Research and Communication Center)
A division of WORLD VISION INTERNATIONAL
919 W. Huntington Drive, Monrovia, CA 91016
Tel. (818) 303-8811

WORLD CHRISTIANITY:
southern africa

Marjorie Froise, editor
Series editor: Edward R. Dayton

ISBN 0-912552-63-8

Printing data: Desktop, in house
                  Typeface: Palatino
                  Edition 1 — 2,500 — 89

Published by:

MARC
(Missions Advanced Research and Communication Center)
A division of WORLD VISION INTERNATIONAL
919 W. Huntington Drive, Monrovia, California, 91016
Tel. (818) 303-8811

In support of the Lausanne Committee
on World Evangelization (LCWE)

9

WORLD CHRISTIANITY SERIES

If we are going to work effectively in the world then we need to know what the world is like. There is no substitute for the hard work of good research well presented.

World Christianity: Southern Africa is a new publication in the WORLD CHRISTIANITY series which is produced by MARC (Missions Advanced Research and Communication Center).

Since 1971, MARC has been preparing "country profiles" and "country portraits" in an effort to keep the freshest possible information before those who plan and strategize for evangelism and mission. These books and booklets have been used in many different ways, at international congresses, in workshops and for private study. When practical, these studies have been published in the form of this book, encompassing a geographical or ethnocultural region.

The researcher and editor of *Southern Africa* is Mrs. Marjorie Froise of Pretoria, South Africa. The study provides factual portraits of South Africa, Botswana, Lesotho, Namibia, and Swaziland.

Mrs. Froise will also be assisting us in the publication of another World Christianity series volume on *South Central Africa*, working with consulting editors from within the countries included or from the region. *South Central Africa* will cover the countries of Angola, Zambia, Zimbabwe, Malawi, and Mozambique.

The work of this volume has been carried on in close cooperation with the Strategy Working Group of the Lausanne Committee for World Evangelization.

Edward R. Dayton
Series Editor

Table of Contents

Historical Background
The Peoples of Botswana
Socioeconomic Conditions
Status of Christianity
Unreached Peoples
National Churches
Foreign Missions
Christian Activities
Needs In Botswana

Historical Background
The Peoples of Lesotho
Socio-economic Conditions
Status of Christianity
Unreached Peoples
National Churches
Foreign Missions
Christian Activities
Needs in Lesotho

Historical Background
The Peoples of Namibia

Socio-economic Conditions
Status of Christianity
Lesser Reached Peoples
National Churches
Christian Activities
Needs in Namibia

Historical Background
Peoples of South Africa
Socioeconomic Characteristics
Status of Christianity
Unreached Peoples
National Churches
Missionary Societies
Christian Activities
Independent and National States
Independent States (Transkei, Bophuthatswana,
   Venda & Ciskei)
National States (Gazankulu, Kangwane, Kwandebele,
   Kwazulu, Lebowa & Quaqwa)

Historical Background
The Peoples of Swaziland
Socio-economic Conditions
Status of Christianity
Unreached Peoples
National Churches
Foreign Missions
Christian Activities
Needs In Swaziland

List of Tables

Swaziland

Addenda

Foreword

When Paul wrote to the Philippians he prayed that their love would abound still more and more in real knowledge and all discernment. The qualities Paul prayed for in the Philippians are equally vital for all in the Church of Christ. In order to minister the gospel of Christ, all Christian workers and organizations need to have "real knowledge and all discernment."

This is especially true in the extraordinarily complex region of Southern Africa where knowing, discerning, understanding and indeed working out our commitments of Christian love and service are unusually demanding. And this applies whether we are structurally involved in church or parachurch frameworks, whether we are contextually situated in urban or rural settings and whether we are practically engaged in evangelism, pastoral work, renewal, social concern, justice issues or whatever.

Wherever we are and whoever we are in God's work in Southern Africa or as overseas people wanting to know more of this region, this reference volume will prove itself a fund of invaluable background information. In fact I believe every Christian minister, lay worker and parachurch leader should have a copy. Encyclopedic work has gone into the research so that a huge array of facts, figures and relevant insights can quickly be brought to the attention of the reader.

The country profiles will also be of assistance in terms of resource to either denominational or parachurch mission strategists who are contemplating new work in outreach or church planting in any of these areas.

Beyond that, teachers, preachers and writers have here much telling statistical data with which to buttress points of affirmation or insight which they may be making.

All in all, we have here a marvelous tool and the editor is to be congratulated for this contribution on the status and progress of Christianity in Southern Africa. May these endeavours help all of us to abound still more and more in real understanding and knowledge as we seek to serve the Lord in our various places of divine appointment.

Michael Cassidy
Founder
African Enterprise
Pietermaritzburg

Acknowledgments

I wish to acknowledge the many people who have assisted me during the period I spent researching for *World Christianity: Southern Africa*. In each of the countries covered in this volume there have been those who have been willing to give of their time to share experiences and insights on their nation, their denomination or organization, as well as perceptions of need within the country in which they live and work.

Others have gone further. They have been willing to review drafts and check information, challenge and make suggestions for improvement. I wish to thank John Nicholson of Life Ministry, and Reverend Joseph Mpakanyana of Global Evangelism Ministry in Lesotho; Doctor Sam Hynd, Reverend Ephraim Dlamini of Swaziland Evangelical Bible Institute in Swaziland and Reverend Don Genheimer of African Evangelical Church in Botswana. In South Africa, Reverend Hugh Wetmore of Evangelical Fellowship of S.A., Reverend Colin Bishop, Professor H.L. Pretorius and World Vision staff members have played a part. In particular I want to thank Sheldon Rankin for his constructive advice. Jeanette James has typed the manuscripts but she has been more than a typiste to me.

Thank you Harald and Linda for allowing me to give of myself to this fulfilling task.

Marjorie Froise
February 1989

Abbreviations

ACAT	Africa Co-operative Action Trust
AEC	African Evangelical Church
AEF	Africa Evangelical Fellowship
AIC	African Independent Churches
ANC	African National Congress
AWB	Afrikaner Weerstandbeweging (an extreme right nationalistic organization)
AZAPO	Azanian People's Organization
°C	degrees Centigrade
COSATU	Congress of South African Trade Unions
DRC	Dutch Reformed Church
ELCIN	Evangelical Lutheran Church in Namibia
est	estimate/d
GDP	Gross Domestic Product
GNP	Gross National Product
HNP	Herstigte Nasionale Party
km	kilometer/s
km^2	kilometers squared
LEC	Lesotho Evangelical Church
LMS	London Missionary Society
mm	millimeter/s
MP	Member of Parliament
NGK	Nederduitse Gereformeerde Kerk (Dutch Reformed Church)
NP	National Party
OMI	Oblates of Mary Immaculate
PEMS	Paris Evangelical Missionary Society
PFP	Progressive Federal Party
prov	provisional
SA	South Africa (or Southern Africa)
SACC	South African Council of Churches
SDA	Seventh Day Adventist
sq	square
SWA	South West Africa (now Namibia)
SWAPO	South West African Peoples' Organization
TBVC	Transkei, Bophuthatswana, Venda & Ciskei
TCC	Transkei Council of Churches
TEAM	The Evangelical Alliance Mission
tech	technical
USA	United States of America
USSR	Union of Soviet Socialist Republics
YMCA	Young Men's Christian Association
YWAM	Youth with a Mission
YWCA	Young Women's Christian Association
WCC	World Council of Churches

INTRODUCTION

World Christianity: Southern Africa is yet another volume in a series of informative publications on the state of the Church in different parts of the world. It endeavors to provide information on churches, missions and parachurch organizations which will assist church leaders to gain a greater understanding of the Church and its ministries.

Political tensions in Southern Africa have held a prominent place in the news in recent years, but this book does not intend to be a political analysis, nor does it offer answers to the problems of this sub-continent. Rather it seeks to tell of what is being done through His Church and His people and to highlight the areas of need in this portion of God's vineyard. In dealing with South Africa, the editor has chosen to utilize given terms, such as Independent and National States, in referring to the ethnic homelands, or "Colored" in referring to people of mixed descent but this does not imply support of such labels or of the system that has generated them.

Research for this volume commenced initially in the World Vision of Southern Africa library, where information on churches and missions in the region is clipped and filed. University libraries, government archives and statistical bulletins, as well as specialized Africana libraries such as the Strange library in Johannesburg, have provided much of the absorbing historical data.

People, however, have provided the bulk of the information for this book. By visiting the countries concerned, I made contact with church leaders and planners and not only have I received needed information but I have had the privilege of sharing in their joys, concerns and hopes for the future. I have felt uplifted but also burdened as I considered the unfinished task.

The Church and its needs

Southern Africa is a land of grandeur and beauty. It is also a land of contrasts which range from sandy deserts to mountain splendor; from symphony orchestras to reed pipes; from urban affluence to rural poverty; from computer-oriented businessmen to people groups untouched by civilization. But there is a thread that draws the more than thirty ethnic groups together -- they all need to experience Christ's redemption and reconciling power in their lives - now more than ever before.

Each of the countries of Southern Africa is so different from the others and yet there is much that is the same; for instance, the **role of women** is similar. Many of the churches throughout the region report that women are in the majority in church membership and in attendance, and their role in the life of the church is becoming increasingly important. Who is reaching the men? A special ministry is needed to reach men who may be living at outlying cattle posts, working as migrants in urban centers, or those who have left God out of their secularized lives.

Are the churches effectively reaching the **young people**? Of the population of thirty-eight million in countries included in this study, thirty-eight percent of the population is under fifteen years of age, while forty-seven percent is under twenty, and yet so many church programs focus their ministry on the middle aged or older segments of the population. We praise God for organizations such as Youth for Christ, Scripture Union and Students' Christian Movement, which are geared to reaching the youth in our region. Is the church ready to integrate these new, youthful believers and provide them with the nurture and encouragement that will help them to grow?

There is a large degree of **nominalism** in the churches. Reports on religious affliation for the region indicate that sixty-two percent of the population claim to be Christian, either Protestant, Catholic or Anglican, while a further twenty-seven percent belong to African Independent Churches. Yet church attendance, in relation to affiliation, does not reflect the same commitment. The people represented by the statistics have all had some contact with the church, be it through mission schooling, hospital care or earlier church attendance. Secularism, disillusionment with the church and its message and irrelevancy, are some of the reasons why members or adherents have drifted away, while many pastors have never been challenged by the need for personal reconciliation with God through the shed blood of Christ and are themselves nominal in their faith.

A clash in worldviews has resulted in **syncretism** in the churches and the proliferation of African Independent Churches. Westerners tend to dichotomize life into sacred and secular, while an African traditional worldview considers life in its totality. In a rural setting, acceptance into the group is generally automatic. Not so in Western culture where the focus is on achievement. The transition from African culture to urbanized Western culture has resulted in a generation of people with major value conflicts. The church has added to the cultural confusion by introducing Western traditions into the church. This conflict of cultures has resulted in the rapid growth of Independent churches whose authentic African expressions of worship blend Christian Biblical beliefs with traditional ancestor veneration in varying degrees. These groups need to be strengthened through Biblical teaching and leadership training.

The prominence of the powerful and prosperous country of **South Africa** has a ripple effect throughout the region. Its positive effects are felt in the provision of labor for many of the residents of its neighbors, the benefits of the customs agreements, and the availability of manufactured goods. Its negative effects are also felt, however, and the legalized discrimination in South Africa creates political refugees in neighboring states. Returning armed insurgents result in South Africa Defence Force forays into these countries, with its resulting destabilization. Furthermore, international economic sanctions and disinvestment also affect the economies of Botswana, Swaziland, Lesotho and Namibia.

The government policies of **discriminatory separate development** have created divisions between black and white and these tensions are currently being felt in the churches where the implications of social and political awareness are being worked out. The Church in South Africa, particularly the ecumenical denominations, is taking a stand against the injustices of government policies and a number of church leaders have become highly politicized. This is resulting in a Church/State confrontation.

Can the Church in South Africa face these challenges? The answer lies in a dynamic encounter with the living God, who holds the nations and His Church in His hand.

Marjorie Froise
Editor
February 1989

CHAPTER ONE

Republic of Botswana:

Third-generation Christianity

REPUBLIC OF BOTSWANA

Profile

Natural Features: 582,000 km^2 (224,711 square miles) of land area occupying a central position in Southern Africa.

Terrain: A flat dry land with a mean altitude of 1,000 meters. The Kalahari (Kgalagadi) desert covers 84% of the land area; the populated eastern area is tree savannah. The Okavango River feeds a huge delta in the northwest.

Climate: Average annual rainfall varies from 650 mm in the northeast to less than 250 mm in the southwest. Rainfall is erratic and unpredictable. Temperatures range from 44°C in summer to below freezing at times in winter.

Population: (1986 estimate) 1,131,700. Annual growth rate: 3.4%. Expatriates comprise 1.6% of the population. Population density: 1.6 per km^2.

Ethnic groups: Batswana, Bakalanga, Basubiya, Hambukushu, San (Bushmen or Basarwa), Bakgalagadi, Bayei and Baherero.

Languages and Literacy: Official languages are Setswana and English. Literacy rate: 35% (school-age children: 65%).

Urbanization: (1986 estimate) 21%. Gaborone, population 96,100, is the capital. Other towns include Francistown (39,600), Lobatse (24,300) and SelebiPikwe (34,700).

Government: A multi-party democracy. The Executive is headed by President Quett Masire. An elected Head of State and Cabinet are responsible to Parliament. The Legislature is a National Assembly elected by the people. The Judiciary administers and interprets the laws of the land. Customary courts handle domestic and local affairs.

Economy: Currency: 100 thebe = 1 Pula (P1 = US $0.59). GDP: P3,300 million (1987). GDP per capita: P2,800. GDP growth rate: 7.9%. Inflation rate: 10% (1986). Imports: P89 million. Exports: P101.4 million (mainly diamonds). Agriculture as a % of GDP: 7.4% (1983).

Religion: Protestant 17%, Roman Catholics 4%, Anglican 1%, African Independent Churches 30%, Traditional religion 37%, Nominal 10%, Marginal Christians and Non-Christians 1%.

Glossary: Botswana, the country; Batswana, the people of the main tribal group (singular Motswana); Setswana, language of the Batswana.

HISTORICAL BACKGROUND

The original inhabitants of Botswana were the San (Bushmen, Basarwa). They had been living in present-day Botswana for thousands of years by the time the Batswana people migrated to the area in the late seventeenth and early eighteenth centuries. Other early entrants into the country were the Bakgalagadi who moved from the Transvaal in the fourteenth century. Both these tribes were either subjugated or pushed further into the Kalahari Desert by the early Tswana immigrants. The tyranny of Shaka Zulu in the nineteenth century resulted in further waves of migration and mass slaughters.

The nineteenth century was a time of unrest and flux as traders, hunters and land speculators converged on the country. Cecil Rhodes had hoped to absorb Botswana into his British South Africa Country; the land-hungry Afrikaner Boers, migrating from the South, had settled along the borders; and the Germans in South West Africa had designs on the area. Chief Khama appealed to the British government and in 1895 the country was named Bechuanaland and became a protectorate of the British government.

The early 1960s saw the formation of the first political parties, the most popular of which was headed by Seretse Khama. In 1965 the first general elections were held and Seretse Khama was elected as the first President. Independence was granted in September 1966, and Bechuanaland became the Republic of Botswana. Seretse Khama proved to be an able and respected leader until his death in 1980.

THE PEOPLES OF BOTSWANA

The **Batswana** comprise 82.5% of the population of Botswana. There are eight principal tribes, seven of whom are Tswana. Three peoples migrated from the Zambezi region the Bayei, Basubia and the Hambukushu. They are river people and settled in the Okavango Delta area. The Kalanga of Shona stock, living in the northeast of the country, were divided from their kin in Zimbabwe when the colonial boundaries were drawn. The Herero people living in the northwest of Botswana moved in from

Namibia at the time of the German revolt. Expatriates number 19,000 or 1.5% of the population.

The San[1] (Basarwa, Bushmen) population is estimated to be 35,000. Their traditional way of life is nomadic and they move camp across borders according to food and water supplies. It is estimated, however, that only 3,000 live exclusively in a hunting/gathering lifestyle. Many San work on cattle-posts or in other forms of employment making adaptations to their lifestyle while still retaining aspects of their traditional way of life.

The population growth rate is high. Improved medical facilities have reduced the infant mortality rate to one of the lowest in Africa. The percentage of the population in the under-fifteen age group is 47%, while 62% of the population is under twenty-five years. Some 80% of the population live in the eastern part of the country.

SOCIOECONOMIC CONDITIONS

At independence, Botswana was one of the poorest countries in the world. Today it has become Africa's success story as mineral treasures have been discovered under its sands. Diamond pipes, discovered after independence, are among the richest in the world and revenue from diamond sales has transformed the economy. Its international reserves in March 1987 equalled more than two years worth of imports.

Agriculture

Although agriculture only contributed 6.3% to the GDP in 1983/84, it nevertheless remains the major source of income for three-quarters of the country's population, and these rural people have not generally benefited from Botswana's growing prosperity. Within the agricultural sector, cattle predominate; yet a survey indicated that 45% of rural homes do not own cattle and that 90% of all dwelling units produced harvests that were inadequate to feed their households (*National Development Plan 1985-91*).

Most households have, nevertheless, benefited from government programs through improved health services, village water supplies and free primary education. Labor-intensive public works schemes are assisting poor rural households.

---

1   Known as *Remote Area Dwellers* in Botswana

Botswana rural homes function around disrupted lifestyles. Families maintain a home in the village where children stay and attend school. The women spend the week on farmlands several kilometers away, while men live at distant cattle-posts for eight months of the year.

Education

Origins of formal schooling in Botswana date back to the early days of missionary endeavor. By the turn of the century 1,000 pupils were being educated in twenty schools. It was not until 1944 that the first secondary school was established. Today it is the government's aim to provide every child with a basic nine-year education aimed at assisting the school leaver to have skills which will lead to self-employment or other productive work. The majority of school-leavers will not find employment in the formal sector.

Health services were hospital based until 1973. Since then a decentralized health care system has been introduced. The Ministry of Health is responsible for health care, but clinics and health posts are operated by communities and local authorities. Community participation in identifying problems is encouraged. Missions operate a total of three hospitals, seven clinics and a dental clinic, and although they are responsible for the running of these health services, they nevertheless cooperate with the centralized health care policies and are partially funded by the government.

Table 1: Social Indicators in Brief

Total enrollment in schools	254,554
% enrollment in primary schools	87%
Total enrolled in secondary schools	12.5%
Total enrolled in tertiary education	5%
Pupil/teacher ratio	30:1
Literacy rate	35%
Literacy rate for schoolage children	65%
Number of hospitals	14
Number of clinics and health posts	348
Population per hospital bed	463
Population per clinic and health post	2,692
Population per doctor	6,000
Population per nurse	602
Infant mortality rate (per 1,000)	79

STATUS OF CHRISTIANITY

There is freedom of religion in Botswana, and the pro-Christian government has introduced Scripture education as a compulsory subject into the school curriculum.

Historical review

The London Missionary Society (LMS) was the first missionary society at the Cape to establish a work in Southern Africa. Jan Kok and William Edwards arrived in 1799 and travelled to Kuruman as agents of LMS where they sought to establish a work amongst the Tswanas. The men lacked funds and spiritual support and after a while they turned to trading and were lost to mission work.

A mission station was later established at Kuruman by James Read and Robert Hamilton and, although it was outside of present-day Batswana country, it became the launching pad for work into present-day Botswana. Robert Moffat arrived in 1820 and spent fifty years of his life reaching Tswana people. The Tswana did not readily respond to the gospel. In fact it was twelve years after commencing work at Kuruman that God's Spirit moved among the people and a number of them began to confess their sin and were baptized. Moffat used the interim years to gain fluency in the language and he began translating the Scriptures until he eventually translated the whole Bible into Setswana. David Livingstone came out to join the Kuruman Mission, married Moffat's daughter Mary, and moved up into present-day Botswana.

The Batswana people were the first Bantu people to hear the gospel in Southern Africa and there was a great response once the chiefs accepted Christianity as the religion of their tribes.

The present situation

Second and third generation Christianity has resulted in a large degree of nominalism in the church. Few mainline churches have any teaching ministry or emphasis on a life of commitment to Christ.

Many members of mainline churches and the majority of those belonging to African Independent Churches have compromising beliefs which allow them to participate in ancestral rituals as well as belong to Christian churches. The question to be asked is whether Biblical Christianity is truly penetrating Tswana traditional way of life. One old man is said to have remarked "Christianity has eaten my head, but not my heart."

Nearly all mainline churches are controlled from outside Botswana, either from South Africa or Zimbabwe, and this presents difficulties. Most churches report that women are in the majority. In some instances female members account for 70-80% of membership. A number of men are working as migrant laborers on the mines in South Africa, while others live at distant cattle posts. These factors contribute to the low percentage of men participating as church members.

A generation of young people is growing up which is prepared to say "I don't belong." Yet there are indications that the youth are open to accept Christianity. Organizations such as Scripture Union are having encouraging results through school club ministry and holiday camps.

Outreach to non-Tswanas is beginning to show results.

A large percentage of Batswana people still consult traditional healers.

UNREACHED PEOPLES

Although the **San** (Bushmen,Basarwa) are identified as a single group of people, over thirty distinct linguistic groups or dialects are known to exist with no *lingua franca*. This makes communication difficult. Many of these people still adhere to a traditional nomadic lifestyle.

A number of churches and missions are seeking to reach the San people. They include the Congregational Church, Lutherans, Dutch Reformed Church, Church of Christ, Africa Evangelical Church and more recently, Charles Haupt Evangelistic Association.

The Bleckmar Mission estimates that 50% of the people have heard about Christ but are unaware of Biblical teaching. They operate seven preaching stations among the San.

Charles Haupt, who has an itinerant ministry, travels to remote cattle posts where small groups of San live. He reports that the people are responsive and ready to accept Christ. Gospel Recording phonettes using the Kang language are left between visits. A further six languages have been recorded by Gospel Recordings.

The **Bakgalagadi** are also nomadic desert people living in the west of the country. This mixed race group is estimated to number 50,000; although, like the San, they are becoming westernized. There is little evangelism being done to reach this specific group of people.

The **Bayei** and **Basubia** people live in the northwestern part of the country and due to communication problems are difficult to reach with the gospel. Although the majority adhere to traditional beliefs, a number have integrated into Tswana churches.

The **Baherero** number about 15,000, the majority of whom live in remote areas. Most of these people identify with the Protestant Unity Church of South West Africa, a syncretistic breakaway from the Lutheran church.

The **Kalanga** people living in northeast Botswana, a population of approximately 75,000, have been difficult to reach with the gospel. Although several mainline churches have congregations among these people, they need a clear presentation of the message of salvation.

Muslims total 2,500 and are mainly Indian traders and professionals. There are mosques at Gaborone and Lobatse. No attempts have been made by the Christian Church to reach them.

There are more than 9,000 **Baha'is** in Botswana, including children. They are found in 210 villages.

NATIONAL CHURCHES

The Botswana government requires that all churches and religious organizations are registered under the provisions of the Societies Act. A total of 192 are listed, including about forty mainline and mission churches. An estimated religious affiliation is listed below.

Table 2: Religious Affiliation in Botswana

Protestants [1]	17%
Roman Catholics [2]	4%
Anglicans	1%
Marginal Christians & non-Christian religions	1%
Nominal	10%
African Independent Churches [1]	30%
Traditional religion [3]	37%

[1] Includes an estimate for children of church-going parents
[2] Membership based on baptism
[3] Residual figure

Membership in various denominations in Botswana is summarized in Table 3.

Table 3: Denominational Membership in Botswana

Lutherans (3 groups)	22,000
United Congregational Church of Southern Africa	20,000
Roman Catholics	44,000
Anglicans	7,000
Seventh Day Adventists	7,000
Assemblies of God	5,000
Dutch Reformed Church in Botswana	4,761
Apostolic Faith Mission	3,239
African Methodist Episcopal Church	3,000
Methodist Church	2,724
Pentecostal Protestant Church	2,000
Pentecostal Holiness Church	2,000

Coordinating bodies

There are three coordinating bodies:

The Botswana Christian Council has thirty-two member churches and organizations, thirteen of whom are African Independent Churches. Much of the aid sent to the country from church affiliated agencies is channelled through the Christian Council.

The *Evangelical Fellowship of Botswana* has fourteen member organizations.

The *Botswana Spiritual Council of Churches* acts as a coordinating body for many of the African Independent Churches.

Roman Catholics

The first attempt to establish a mission station in Botswana was in 1879 when eleven Jesuits set out to reach the Zambezi and establish a base at Shoshong. However, two of their number died and the enterprise was abandoned.

The second effort was in the first quarter of the century when five Oblate Fathers moved up from the south, but the biggest obstacle they faced was the determination of the London Missionary Society to keep them out, and they were refused permission to stay. The first firm foundation was laid in 1928 at Kgale by German oblates and later missions were established at Lobatse and Ramotswa.

When the Irish Passionist priests arrived in 1952 led by Father Murphy, a missionary priest, there were about 1,000 Catholics. Since then the work has grown fast. Bechuanaland was constituted a Prefecture Apostolic in the care of the Passionist Congregation in 1959. At Independence in 1966, Father Murphy became the first bishop of the newly appointed Diocese of Gaborone under the province of Bloemfontein.

Today there is an estimated Catholic population of 44,000. Although all but four of the thirty-five priests are expatriates (including two Ghanians) the Bishop of Gaborone, Right Reverend Bishop Boniface Setlalekgosisi, is a Motswana. There are twenty-one parishes with sixty-one outstations.

The Catholic church established twelve schools, two medical clinics and six adult educational centers. Thirteen convents are situated across the country. A minor seminary was recently opened.

The Catholic church has a service called "Priest on Tour." A priest spends his time travelling across the remote parts of the country, offering the sacraments, Christian literature, and simple health care.

In 1959 Botswana became an ecclesiastical unit with the title "Prefecture Apostolic of the Protectorate."

Anglican Church

The Anglican Church began its work in Botswana in 1885 primarily to minister to its own members who had emigrated to Botswana. The Railway Mission was established to reach Batswana along the train route, and work was established in the north by the Diocese of Kuruman and Kimberley. Efforts to expand were hampered by the chiefs who felt that one church, invariably the London Missionary Society, was adequate to meet the needs of their people, and this made expansion difficult.

In 1957 an invitation was given by the chief of the Bamangwato to work in his area if they would also undertake social activities, and in 1959 the Mmadinare Mission was opened, and a clinic and hospital established.

Today the Anglican Church in Botswana is one Diocese under the Central African Office. There are an estimated 7,000 church members worshipping in twelve churches. Seventeen ministers, the majority of whom are expatriate, minister to these congregations.

Protestant churches

United Congregational Church of Southern Africa

The London Missionary Society's mission stations at Kuruman is where the Congregational Church in Botswana had its roots. Robert Moffat devoted fifty years of his life to reaching the Batswana people, providing schooling and translating the Scriptures into Setswana. In fact, the first Motswana to be ordained as a minister in 1911 was trained at Kuruman mission.

David Livingstone was the first to establish a permanent mission within present-day Botswana. John Mackenzie and Roger Price figured prominently in the spread of Christianity across Botswana. By 1880 the London Missionary Society was well established among the Tswana tribes.

The London Missionary Society united with other churches to form the United Congregational Church of Southern Africa in 1967 and today Congregational Churches are to be found scattered across Botswana, reaching into remote areas. The number of members is estimated to be approximately 20,000 worshipping in ninety-five churches and many preaching points. There are only four aging full-time pastors and although there are men in training for the ministry, they do not anticipate serving the churches in a full-time capacity because of financial constraints. The church has been autonomous since 1980.

Lutheran Church

The first Lutheran contact with Botswana was in 1862 when Reverend Schulenberg of the Hermannsburg Mission baptized Khama II, the Paramount Chief of the Bangwato people. Unfortunately, this breakthrough by the Lutherans was never consolidated; the missionaries withdrew from the Bangwato area leaving the London Missionary Society to fill the gap.

Hermannsberg Mission continued, however, to build up their work in the southeastern corner of the country. The Berlin Mission was a relative latecomer to the scene. Their work commenced in 1951. In 1972, the Bleckman Mission, together with the Lutheran Church of Southern Africa, initiated a program of outreach into Botswana which grew rapidly.

Today there are three Lutheran groupings:

The *Evangelical Lutheran Church in Botswana* with 14,400 members who came together in 1978 from churches originally formed by the German Missions. It is an autonomous church supported through finance and personnel by European partners. It has recently established its own seminary which currently has nine students. The church is deeply involved in social outreach through drought relief, educational and literacy programs and other programs.

The *Evangelical Lutheran Church of Southern Africa* has 7,000 members and is a diocese of the Evangelical Lutheran Church of Southern Africa. Talks are underway to combine these two Lutheran groups.

The *Bleckman Mission* has 5,500 members in eleven churches.

Dutch Reformed Church in Botswana

Work amongst the Batswana began in 1864 at Saulspoort in the Transvaal. Schools were established and converts baptized, but clashes between the Chief and the Afrikaners gave rise to a mass migration of the people to Mochudi within the Botswana borders. In 1874 a young missionary visited Mochudi and permission was given for him to settle there, which he did in 1877. The most momentous event in the history of the tribe was when the Chief became a Christian in 1892. The Chief's act made a lasting impression on the people, and many of them followed his example. In effect, the Dutch Reformed Church became the national church of the Bakgatla people.

In 1979, a union of the Dutch Reformed Church, the Dutch Reformed Church in Africa, and the Dutch Reformed Mission Church resulted in the Dutch Reformed Church in Botswana which is independent of the Church in South Africa. They have nearly 5,000 members in seven congregations. A Bible School is operating at Gaborone.

A 130-bed hospital at Mochudi with specialist eye treatment continues to function at Mochudi. A blind rehabilitation center is funded by the Christoffel Blinden Mission.

There are seven ministers, two of whom are expatriate.

African Independent Churches

There are approximately 160 African Independent (AIC) Churches in Botswana, most of whom have official registration. Of these groups about half are of apostolic tradition. Most of the leadership is untrained and many of the pastors are illiterate. Since their theology is unwritten it is difficult to define, but generally it includes Christian beliefs mingled with ancestral traditions in varying degrees.

These churches generally appeal to older people and there is a higher percentage of men in these churches than in mainline churches. This is possibly because the hierarchical system offers men status which is not available in mainline churches.

Mennonite missionaries have a Bible-training ministry among these people which is based mainly on oral communication. Despite the fact that many AIC leaders are illiterate, a number of them memorize Scripture. It is felt that there are regenerate Christians in these church groups.

These churches include:

- Eleven Apostles Healing Church
- New Apostolic Prophets Church
- Spiritual Healing Church
- Saint Faith Holy Church
- Saint Philip's Faith Healing Church
- Zion Christian Church

FOREIGN MISSIONS

There are between twenty and thirty missionary societies and parachurch organizations operating in Botswana. Many of the expatriate missionaries are working with national churches which have grown out of their work. The parachurch organizations comprise service agencies as well as those involved in evangelism. They include:

- Africa Evangelical Fellowship
- Baptist Mission of Botswana
- Campus Crusade for Christ
- Christian Missions in Many Lands
- Christoffel Blindenmission
- Church of God
- Church of the Nazarene
- Holiness Union Mission
- Lutheran World Federation
- Mennonite Ministries
- Scripture Union
- Seventh Day Adventists
- Youth with a Mission

Flying Mission, an indigenous service organization, operates four aircraft. Its services are used by the Ministry of Health as well as Christian organizations.

It is estimated that there are between 150 and 200 expatriate missionaries and Christian workers in Botswana.

CHRISTIAN ACTIVITIES

Evangelism

Early in the history of the church in Botswana many people turned to Christ when their chiefs accepted Christianity. One dramatic breakthrough was in 1862 when a Lutheran missionary baptized Khama III, Paramount Chief of the Ngwato people.

Today the church is again in need of revival; although people are hearing the message of salvation and turning to Christ, the numbers are few.

Scripture Union is having an effective ministry among the young people. Full-time workers are needed to meet the tremendous need and to disciple new believers.

Youth with a Mission, working from Selebe Pikwe mainly among Tswana people, are reaching the churched and the unchurched for Christ.

Organizations involved in evangelism include: Charles Haupt Ministries, reaching out to San and Khalagadi people; Every Home Crusade; and Christ for All Nations.

Broadcasting

The Church Radio Council, an interdenominational group of churches, is responsible for all religious broadcasts over Radio Botswana. Broadcasts from radio stations in South Africa and Bophuthatswana can be heard and Setswana broadcasts from Trans World Radio are a further possibility for those seeking to hear the Word of God.

Literature and Bible distribution

Robert Moffat considered Bible translation to be his life's priority. He taught the Tswana people to read, translated the Bible into their language and in 1857 printed 2,000 copies of the complete Tswana Bible on his press at Kuruman which had been brought to the area by ox wagon. This publication was the first Bible to be printed in an African language.

The Living Bible is currently being translated into Setswana. In 1985 the Bible Society distributed 17,000 Bibles, 1,280 New Testaments, and 8,000 portions of Scripture. Kalanga and Herero languages have translations in progress. Portions of Scripture are also available in Kang.

A number of Christian organizations distribute literature and these include the Flying Mission, who distribute Good News Bibles as well as other Christian literature, Youth With A Mission and Scripture Union.

The Africa Evangelical Church operates a bookshop in Gaborone, Lesedi Christian Centre, and there are several other small outlets for Christian literature. There is a need for Christian literature to be published in Setswana.

The Baha'i religion has seen the need for literature in the vernacular and is translating their training material into Setswana.

Christian education

Compulsory religious education is part of the school curriculum. The content of the syllabus is decided by a committee which has representatives from Christian organizations including Scripture Union and the Dutch Reformed Church.

A number of church and parachurch groups have non-formal study courses, such as the Bibleway study course conducted by the Baptist Mission. Scripture Union also offers training material as a follow-up.

Seminaries, Bible Colleges, and training centers include:

- Assembly of God Bible College at Tlokweng
- Botswana Bible Training Institute
- Dutch Reformed Church Theological School in Gaborone
- Marang Minor Theological Seminary (Roman Catholic)
- Shashe Bible Training College (Africa Evangelical Church)
- Theological Seminary (Evangelical Lutheran Church in Botswana)
- Theological Training Program (an ecumenical program supported by a number of churches)

Social concerns

Drought in Botswana is a continuing hazard and aid is needed for impoverished and drought-affected people. Development schemes to assist people to become self-sufficient are being implemented by a number of parachurch and mission groups.

They include:

- Botswana Christian Council
- Christoffel Blindenmission
- Church World Services
- Lutheran World Federation
- Mennonite Central Committee
- Roman Catholic Church
- Seventh Day Adventists
- World Vision International

Although overall responsibility for health care is the responsibility of the government, a number of missions and churches are involved in providing health care. These include:

- Anglican hospital at Mmadinare
- Bamalete Lutheran Hospital in Ramotswa
- Dutch Reformed Church Hospital at Mochudi
- Seventh Day Adventist Hospital at Kanye

The Africa Evangelical Church operates an agricultural program at Shashe.

The Evangelical Lutheran Church in Botswana is involved in drought relief, educational programs, rehabilitation for the disabled and youth programs.

NEEDS IN BOTSWANA

The church in Botswana has become a nominal church. It needs a spiritual awakening leading to committed and renewed lives.

The ratio of women in the churches in relation to men is disproportionate. Ministries for two groups of men are required: urbanized men involved in commerce and industry, and rural men living at isolated cattle posts for most of the year.

With 62% of the population in the under twenty-five age bracket, the church will need to plan new strategies geared to reaching this age group.

There is a need for Christian literature in Setswana.

Non-Tswana peoples living in remote areas are difficult to reach and have no Scripture in their languages. The challenge of these unreached people groups must be owned by the local church.

Muslim and Baha'i are not seen by the churches in Botswana as groups that need to be evangelized.

BIBLIOGRAPHY

Africa South of the Sahara 1986, Europa Publications.

Barrett, David, *World Christian Encyclopedia*.

Botswana Government Gazette, 24 May, 1985 & 24 January, 1986, Government Printer.

Butler, Alan, *Kuruman Moffatt Mission*, Kuruman Moffat Mission Trust.

ByaruhangaAkiiki, A.B.T., *Tswana Religion vis a vis World Religion*, University of Botswana.

ByaruhangaAkiiki, A.B.T., *Empirical Data on Religion in Botswana, Comparative Studies of the Objectives of 14 Religious Societies in Botswana*, University of Botswana.

Fako, Thabo T., *A guide to the Registered Churches in Botswana*, University of Botswana.

Millar, Laila, *An Introduction to Religion and Churches in Botswana*, Mennonite Central Committee.

Ministry of Finance & Development Planning, *National Development Plan 1985-91*.

Religious Tract Society, *Rivers of Water in a Dry Place: The Introduction of Christianity into South Africa*.

Waldron, Derek, *The Churches Say Yes*, Society for the Propagation of the Gospel, 1961.

CHAPTER TWO

Kingdom of Lesotho:

Needs Beyond Tradition

KINGDOM OF LESOTHO

Profile

Natural Features: 30,355 km^2 (11,720 sq miles) of land area. It forms a tiny enclave within the Republic of South Africa.

Terrain: Mountain ranges cover 85% of the country. A 50 km wide lowland belt lies west of the mountains and is the main agricultural zone. Altitudes in the lowlands average between 1,500 and 1,800 meters.

Climate: Temperate with summer rainfall. Frost is present most of the year in the mountains with snow in winter. Temperatures range from 30°C in summer in the lowlands to -15°C in the mountains in winter.

Population: (1986 estimate) 1,577,000. Annual growth rate: 2.6%. Population density: 51 per km^2 (92 per km^2 in the lowlands, 18 per km^2 in the mountains)

Ethnic groups: Basotho 93%, Nguni (Zulu and Xhosa) 6%, expatriates 1% (whites and Asian traders).

Languages and Literacy: Official languages are Sesotho and English. Literacy rate is 65%.

Urbanization: 16%. Urban Centers: Maseru (population 106,000) is the capital. Other towns are Teyateyaneng, Mafeteng, Leribe, Mohale's Hoek, and Quthing.

Government: A military council is headed by Major-General Justin Lekhanya. The constitutional monarch and Head of State is King Moshoeshoe II. The country is divided into ten administrative districts.

Economy: (1986) Currency: 100 Lisente = 1 Loti (plural Maloti); 1 Loti = US $0.45 (July 1988); on a par with the South African Rand. GDP: M684 million. GNP: M1,298 million. The difference between GDP and GNP represents migrant wages. GDP per capita: M434 (This figure rises to M823 per capita if migrant wages are included). Inflation rate: 16%. Imports: M815 million. Exports: M56 million. Agriculture as % of GDP: 20% (1986/87).

Religion: Roman Catholic 49%, Protestant 15%, Anglican 5%, African Independent Churches 9%, Traditional 7%, Nominal and other 15%.

Glossary: Lesotho, the country; Basotho, the people of Lesotho (singular - Mosothu); Sesotho, the language of the Basotho people.

HISTORICAL BACKGROUND

Lesotho was sparsely populated by San (Bushmen, Basarwa) until the early seventeenth century when southward migrating tribes gradually started settling in the area. The wars of Shaka Zulu in the nineteenth century fragmented this settlement of people. Moshoeshoe I gathered together remnants of the scattered Basotho tribes and about 1820 a nation emerged.

Moshoeshoe was an outstanding leader and for many years was able to withstand warring black tribes as well as conquer others. However, under intense pressure from the Afrikaner *boers* he was forced to accept the protection of the British government. The original inhabitants, the San, were either killed or fled, so that today no San are found in Lesotho.

In 1910 an advisory Basotoland Council was formed with a British High Commissioner as President of the Council. In 1955 they were granted legislative powers and in 1966 Basotoland was granted full independence under King Moshoeshoe II, with legislative power vested in a parliament. The name of the country was changed to Lesotho.

Chief Leabua Jonathan became the first Prime Minister and twenty years of iron-fisted rule followed. When his power was threatened he banned the opposition party and suspended the constitution; King Moshoeshoe fled into exile for a period. Ties with the USSR, China, North Korea and Eastern-bloc countries were established and relationships between Lesotho and South Africa became strained.

In January 1986, a military coup toppled Leabua Jonathan and his government, and the newly established military council handed over executive and legislative power to King Moshoeshoe.

THE PEOPLES OF LESOTHO

Lesotho is occupied predominantly by Basotho people, and although Xhosa people live in the south (over the border from

Transkei) and Zulu people live in the north (over the border from KwaZulu), their numbers are difficult to gauge since the government classifies them as Basotho people, and all education is in Sesotho. The small group of whites live in the major towns and are involved in industry, commerce or development programs.

The mountain people are less westernized because of their geographical isolation. Airstrips are dotted across the mountains with small aircrafts being the major means of communication. Mountain towns are accessible by four-wheel drive vehicles. Transport into outlying districts is by mountain pony.

SOCIO-ECONOMIC CONDITIONS

Lesotho, one of the world's least developed countries, is dependent on the Republic of South Africa. Revenue reflects this dependency with the South African Customs Union providing no less than 60% of the 1985/86 budget. Furthermore, a large proportion of the Gross National Product is derived from migrant wages - South Africa employs some 60% of the male labor force. Job creation within Lesotho is one of the country's top priority needs.

The migrant labor system has had a profound effect on family life in Lesotho, resulting in households headed by women. This in turn has ahd an effect on the new generation of young people who question Christianity and their role in life. Social ills such as prostitution and alcoholism are rife.

Since independence, large sums of money have been poured into Lesotho by donor nations and agencies, but the persistence of development problems and aid dependency give rise to uncertainty among donor nations as to the effectiveness of their aid.

Agriculture

Only 9% of the land is arable. Agriculture employs about 80% of the resident labor force, but only 30% of production is marketed. Yields are low. The land is overstocked by 300% resulting in serious soil erosion problems. Grazing land is communally owned, but arable land is allocated to individuals and families by the chiefs. The earnings of migrant laborers far exceeds possible returns from other sources; as a result, the people are moving from a subsistence agriculture base to a cash economy.

Education and health

Missions and churches developed the school system, but the government is gradually assuming greater control.

The churches have also played an important role in the health care system and continue to do so. Missionary Aviation Fellowship, on contract to the government, flies medical personnel to remote clinics, particularly in the mountains. Over the past decade the emphasis has shifted from curative medicine to preventive health care.

Table 1: Social Indicators in Brief

Total enrollment in education in 1981	287,468
% enrollment in primary education	90.1%
% enrolled in secondary schools	9.0%
% enrolled in tech/vocational training	0.5%
% enrolled in university	0.4%
Literacy rate (1984)	65%
Pupil/teacher ratio	48:1
Number of hospitals	20
Number of clinics	93
Population per hospital bed	607
Population per hospital & clinic	13,955
Population per doctor	12,265
Population per nurse	3,090
Population per witch doctor/herbalist	150

STATUS OF CHRISTIANITY

Lesotho is considered to be a Christian country with a large percentage of the population claiming allegiance to a Christian denomination. However, growth in church membership is not keeping up with the high population growth rate and the percentage of the population with church affiliation is declining. The overwhelming majority of Christians belong to the Roman Catholic church.

Historical review

The entrance of Christianity into the country dates back to 1833. Chief Moshoeshoe, the leader of the Basotho people, was subject to incessant raids by numerous enemies. Furthermore his grandfather had been eaten by cannibals. He sent for a professional hunter who had travelled his country asking him if he knew of any 'medicine' that would protect him from the marauding tribes. The hunter, Krotz, told him of missionaries who could bring peace to his land. On hearing this, Moshoeshoe requested that Krotz buy him a servant of God for his own use and sent a herd of cattle to secure one. And so it was that three French missionaries en route to Bechuanaland were asked to consider ministering in the country of Moshoeshoe. "We should have made an unforgivable mistake," they wrote afterwards to their directors, "if we had refused such a remarkable call." Moshoeshoe directed them in their choice of site and the first mission station of the Paris Evangelical Missionary Society was established at Morija.

The churches' approach to evangelizing the Basotho nation was through education and health care, and through these institutional methods church membership grew rapidly.

Lesotho is possibly one of the earliest countries in Africa to have sent missionaries to other countries. In 1844 Reverend Allison of the Wesleyan Methodist Church took two Basotho teachers to respond to a call from King Mswati of Swaziland. A tract of land was given them and the Mosotho men were left to establish the work. When he returned a year later, adults and children were able to read and two men were ready to accept Christ. Francois Coillard of the Paris Evangelical Mission included three Basotho evangelists in his party when he left Basotoland to establish a pioneer work among the Lozi people in Zambia in 1885.

The present situation

A considerable proportion of church members are regular churchgoers but their Christianity is very nominal with little commitment. Church membership is necessary for baptisms, marriage and funerals and to a large degree Westernized Christianity has become a culture replacing or mingling with traditional ancestral beliefs.

The churchgoers consist mainly of women and children since the majority of the men are working in South Africa on contract. This presents leadership difficulties in the church and it is expected that women will play a prominent role in church leadership in the future.

The youth, especially in mainline denominations, are becoming disillusioned with Christianity. Some are hoping to find reality and re-establish contact with their lost culture through the Black Consciousness movement. The smaller evangelical church groups, however, report an increase in interest among the young people.

There are few full-time ministers in Protestant churches in Lesotho, and many of those who are working full-time are financed from outside of the country. Poverty within the country, the absence of working males and an evident aid dependency are contributing factors.

UNREACHED PEOPLES

Muslims of Asian descent operate as traders and professionals particularly in the north. A mosque is situated at Butha Buthe. Muslims are attempting to spread their faith among the national people. The estimated Muslim population is 1,500.

Baha'i operate in 531 localities in Lesotho and have an estimated 4,500 adherents.

Mountain People are less reached because of their isolation. The established mountain towns have a good representation of Catholic and Protestant churches, with many outstations extending into the isolated areas, but communication is poor and the only access to remote settlements is by mountain pony. Despite the presence of churches and their outstations, traditional ancestral veneration or adherence to syncretistic independent churches is prevalent.

NATIONAL CHURCHES

The estimated religious affiliation is listed below:

Table 2: Religious Affiliation in Lesotho

Roman Catholics [1]	49%
Protestants [2]	15%
Anglican [1]	5%
African Independent Churches [2]	9%
Traditional religion [3]	7%
Nominal & other [4]	15%

[1] Includes baptized children
[2] Includes an estimate for children of church-going parents
[3] Estimate
[4] Residual figure

Denominational membership in the larger denominations is summarized in Table 3.

Table 3: Denominational Membership in Lesotho

Roman Catholics (1985)	771,583
Lesotho Evangelical Church	91,696
Church of the Province of Southern Africa *(Anglican)*	80,000
Assemblies of God	5,000
Apostolic Faith Mission	1,000
Methodist Church of Southern Africa	5,770
Dutch Reformed Church in Africa	5,068
Full Gospel Church of God	1,173
Church of God	5,000
Seventh Day Adventist	2,000
African Methodist Episcopal Church	7,319
Mahon Mission (Baptist)	1,000
Africa Independent Churches *(estimate)*	100,000

Smaller groups include the Baptist Mission, Church of the Bible Covenant, National Baptist Convention, Salvation Army, and Maseru United Church.

Christian Council of Lesotho was established in 1964 and has five member churches:

- African Methodist Episcopal Church
- Church of the Province of Southern Africa
- Lesotho Evangelical Church Methodist Church of Southern Africa
- Roman Catholic Church

The Council meets regularly with the government to discuss matters of mutual interest.   Its main concerns are rural and community development programs.

As a unifying body the Christian Council does not appear to be effective. Its small membership is partly due to the churches' inability to pay the annual dues.

Roman Catholics

The Catholics started work in 1862 with the arrival of Bishop Allard and other members of his French religious order, the Oblates of Mary Immaculate (OMI). They were accompanied by sisters of the Order of Visitation.   They established their headquarters close to the mountain fortress of Moshoeshoe in the area now called Roma.

Initially progress was slow but the devotion of the oblates and sisters, the large amounts of funds invested from overseas and the establishment of schools and clinics resulted in rapid growth. The conversion of the house of Moshoeshoe greatly enhanced their importance in the country.

In 1930 the work was handed over to Canadian OMI missionaries. At that time the church membership totalled 60,000. By 1953, the Catholic community had grown to 205,000. In 1985 the figure was 771,583.

Development of the Roman Catholic Church

1894   Became a Prefecture under the Natal Vicariate
1909   Constituted as a Vicariate
1952   Diocese of Maseru established under the Hierarchy of Southern Africa
1961   Ecclesiastical Hierarchy established with Maseru as the Metropolitan See
1961-78 Diocese at Leribe, Qachas Nek, and Mohale's Hoek were established

The first Basotho priest was ordained in 1930. Today there are sixty Basotho priests out of a total of 124. Since 1981 there has been an increased interest in training for the ministry. The majority of priests, both national and expatriate, belong to the OMI religious order.

The Charismatic renewal movement is active in a few churches.

The Roman Catholic Church is deeply involved in serving the community. It operates forty-eight high schools, twelve hospitals and health care centers as well as numerous clinics. Primary schools, now taken over by the Department of Education, numbered more than 400.

The Lesotho Catholic Bishops' Conference was established in 1972. Through its various commissions it oversees religious and missionary endeavor, health, development and social welfare.

Many religious orders are working in Lesotho in a total of eighty-one convents. They include:

- Daughters of Charity
- Good Shepherd Sisters
- Handmaids of Christ the Priest
- Holy Family Sisters
- Salesian Sisters
- Servants of Christ the Priest
- Sisters of Charity
- Sisters of Saint Joseph
- Sisters of the Holy Name

Priests are trained at Saint Augustine's Seminary and catechists are trained at the Pastoral Catechetical Training Center, both of which are situated at Roma. Aid and development programs are backed by Caritas Lesotho and Catholic Relief Services.

Protestant churches

Lesotho Evangelical Church (LEC)

At the request of Chief Moshoeshoe, three missionaries of the Paris Evangelical Missionary Society (PEMS) arrived in 1833 to commence a ministry among the Basotho people. The progress of the work was initially very slow and it was six years before any conversions were recorded. The early years were well spent in acquiring a thorough knowledge of the language, starting small schools, writing booklets and translating portions of Scripture. In 1841 the first printing press was introduced.

The history of the mission is interwoven with that of the country. Strife between the Dutch and the Basotho in the 50's and 60's did little to help the cause of the mission. The missionaries were not discouraged however and by 1871 there were 1,331 converts and 1,430 candidates for baptism. The school work was also growing and a teachers training college was established. Outstations were being opened and by 1883 there were 126 out-stations, each one in the care of a national evangelist.

It was not until 1898 that the *Seboka*, a mixed assembly of missionaries and Basotho ministers was established, after which the work was referred to as the Church of Basotoland. At the same time as the work was expanding within the country, so the vision to reach other tribes became a reality.

In 1964 the church resulting from the work of the PEMS came of age, becoming the Lesotho Evangelical Church (LEC). The church was divided into parishes and presbyteries and laymen were given equal representation with clergy. Closer ties with other churches were sought and in 1965 the LEC became a founding member of the Lesotho Christian Council.

The numerical growth as well as social work of the church has been hampered through the years because of lack of finance but it has nevertheless remained the largest Protestant denomination.

Year	Members
1904	40,965 (including children)
1935	31,979
1970	65,822
1983	91,696 (101,044 including children)

In 1983 there were fifty-seven ministers and 342 evangelists working in sixty-three parishes and outstations. A presbytery with seven churches is operating in South Africa to reach the migrant mine workers.

The church remains heavily involved in the education system and in 1981, 103,000 pupils were enrolled in LEC schools. The number of secondary schools has increased from ten in 1971 to thirty-three in 1983.

Health care has progressively shifted from curative medicine to preventive health care; two hospitals and a health center train village workers to identify health needs in their community.

Dutch Reformed Church

The Dutch Reformed Church in Africa, working across the border in the Orange Free State, felt a concern for their fellow-Basotho in Lesotho, and a work was commenced as a joint undertaking between the Dutch Reformed Church in Africa and the white Dutch Reformed Church. Three white missionaries were allocated to mission work supported by black evangelists. The first Mosotho minister accepted a call to the church in Maseru in 1976. By 1981 there were seven congregations with a total of 5,068 members and adherents. These churches remain under the regional synod of the Orange Free State in South Africa.

Methodist Church

Missionaries of the Wesleyan Methodist Missionary Society secured land concessions from Chief Moshoeshoe in 1833 and commenced work among the Barolong people west of the Caledon River, and by the end of 1834 work had began among two sub-groups and the mixed race Griqua people. However, this territory was annexed by the Orange Free State in 1866 and is no longer part of Lesotho.

Work in Basotoland itself did not begin until much later. In fact it was not until 1927 that the first Methodist minister was appointed to Mafeteng. After a slow start, the work has now grown to 5,770 full and on-trial members worshipping in five circuits.

A hospital was opened in 1981 at Semongkong in the mountains. They also run a vocational school and a primary school.

African Methodist Episcopal Church

African Methodist Episcopal church has seventy-eight churches with a membership of 7,319. There is generally a pastor for each church but not all pastors are trained and few are involved in full time ministry.

Pentecostal churches

There are three main Pentecostal groups:

Assemblies of God of Lesotho have thirty-six congregations. They run a Bible School in Maseru and a clinic and high school at Mount Tabor.

Apostolic Faith Mission has fifteen congregations, sixteen pastors and approximately 1,000 members. It operates an evangelistic arm, Christ Mobile Unit. One full-time evangelist conducts tent missions throughout Lesotho.

Full Gospel Church of God, with twenty-eight churches and 1,173 members, are working to the north of the country where they operate a small Bible School.

Anglican Church

The Anglican church in Lesotho is a Diocese of the Church of the Province of Southern Africa.

In 1850 Moshoeshoe came to hear of the 'English Church' and sent a message to Bishop Gray in Cape Town asking him to visit him and send 'English teachers' to his country. Bishop Gray was unable to visit him in person but promised that he would send him clergy as soon as possible. The promise was fulfilled, but not until after Moshoeshoe's death.

Moshoeshoe, however, took the opportunity of sending two of his sons to an Anglican School in the Cape. One of his sons, Libopuoa, was baptized and confirmed and requested training for the priesthood. He was sent to St Augustine's in Canterbury for training, but died of pneumonia.

In 1875 work was established at Mohale's Hoek in the south and Leribe in the north. Today there are fifty-three clergy of whom only nine are ex-patriates. They minister in twenty-six parishes and approximately 300 outstations.

Priests are trained at Lelapa La Jesu Seminary at the National University of Lesotho.

Three religious communities are working in Lesotho:

- Community of the Holy Name for Women
- Society of the Precious Blood for Women
- The Society of the Sacred Mission for Laymen and Priests

Other institutions include:

- Saint James Mission Hospital at Mantsonyane
- Eighteen secondary and high schools
- Craft Center School
- An agricultural secondary school

Membership in 1987 was estimated to be 80,000.

African Independent Churches

There are approximately 200 Independent Churches in Lesotho, eighty-two of which are registered with the government. Most of these groups are syncretistic. Their numbers range from larger groups such as the Kereke ea Moshoeshoe with approximately 6,000 members, to small groups with ten to twenty members. It is estimated that there are 100,000 affiliated to Independent Churches. Few of these groups have church buildings. The African Federal Church Council links about thirty of these churches together.

Some of the larger groups include:

- Apostolic Church in Zion of the New Jerusalem
- Kereke ea Moshoeshoe
- Zion Christian Church
- Zion Foundation Church of Lesotho

Africa Inter-Mennonite Mission is involved in theological education and leadership training among these people.

FOREIGN MISSIONS

The history of Christianity in Lesotho has evolved from 'Missions' to 'Churches of the missions.' The expatriate Protestant missionaries working in Lesotho are involved either in a support role to national churches or in specialist parachurch organizations. At present there are approximately seventy mission societies or parachurch organizations represented in Lesotho, with between 150-200 missionaries. In some instances the work commenced by missionary societies or parachurch agencies is now operating under national leadership. In addition a number of indigenous evangelistic and parachurch groups have developed.

CHRISTIAN ACTIVITIES

Evangelism

The large degree of nominalism in this Christian country is of great concern to evangelicals in Lesotho. Special ministries of established churches, especially the pentecostal groups, are beginning to show results. One national pastor aptly phrased his hopes when he said "little doors are opening."

The Apostolic Faith Mission has a full-time evangelist involved in an itinerant tent ministry.

A group of eighteen churches and parachurch organizations has grouped together to form Network of Love, and although its primary aim is emergency relief, evangelistic efforts have resulted in 15,000 responding to appeals to receive Christ in fourteen locations. A warm response has been shown to follow-up and teaching.

Scripture Union is involved in evangelism through high schools and camp ministry. Discipleship groups have been formed.

Campus Crusade (local name: Life Ministry) is active in lay training and seminars as well as outreach at the National University of Lesotho and the National Teachers Training College. The Jesus Film has been extensively used as an evangelism tool since 1982. It has now been translated into Sesotho (sponsored by Missionary Aviation Fellowship).

Global Evangelism Ministries have an open door into Lesotho prisons. They praise God for changed lives. Evangelistic campaigns, followed by correspondence Bible study courses, evidence encouraging results. Every Home Crusade is a six-year program aimed at reaching 250,000 households with the gospel. To date 37,000 homes have been reached, 11,000 have returned the response form and 4,000 have completed the first Bible study course. Outreach into schools, the Teacher Training College and the University is undertaken.

Hospital Christian Fellowship is active in Maseru and some district hospitals. It focuses on Christian training, evangelism in wards and small group discipleship Bible studies.

Broadcasting

Religious programs on Radio Lesotho began in 1968. Time is allocated daily on a denominational basis at no cost. Ten minutes of prayer each morning and evening opens and closes daily transmissions and, in addition, time for religious broadcasts is granted during the day.

Transmissions from South Africa which include religious broadcasts can be picked up. Trans World Radio, operating from Swaziland, also broadcasts in the Sesotho language.

Literature

Lesotho has a long history of religious publishing. The Lesotho Evangelical Church Press at Morija, established in 1841, played an important role in the printing of Scripture portions in the last century. Today it publishes the church newspaper, *Leselinyana La Lesotho*, as well as church and educational material.

The Roman Catholic Church likewise has been involved in printing religious material at its press and publishing house at Mazenod. Today they produce a weekly church newspaper, *Moeletsi Oa Basotho*, as well as religious and educational material. Twenty-four bookshops operate throughout the country.

Currently, Global Evangelism Ministry is assisting in religious instruction programs in schools using posters and accompanying tracts with a tear off slip offering a free Bible study. Half a million tracts are distributed annually, as well as Scripture portions. Christian literature is included in packs of food aid distributed by evangelism teams and evangelical development workers.

Literature in Sesotho remains the best language medium for reaching the lower classes. English could be used to reach the upper and middle classes. There is a need for culturally acceptable material to reach these two latter groups. Locally produced material in Sesotho is scant, most of it produced by missionaries a number of years ago. There is a need for literature which will give Christian responses to felt needs and problems in the community.

Literature could be used more effectively as a means of evangelism. Because of the high literacy rate, particularly among the young people, literature is gratefully accepted and read.

Bible translation and distribution

Reverend Arbousset of the Paris Evangelical Missionary Society translated portions of Scripture into Sesotho. The gospels of Mark and Luke were printed in Cape Town in 1839. The New Testament was completed in 1855 and the whole Bible in 1881. This translation was revised in 1946. A new translation of the Bible is underway and is expected to be published in 1988. The New Testament and Psalms of this translation was available in 1976. Small groups of Xhosa and Zulu populations have the whole Bible in their languages.

The Bible Society in Lesotho was inaugurated in 1967. In 1985 a total of 28,032 Scripture items was distributed which included

6,401 Bibles, 5,576 New Testaments and 15,772 portions. The demand for subsidized Scriptures remains high.

Christian education

The first training center to be established was the Morija Training Institution which had its beginnings in 1869. It trained young men as ministers, evangelists or school teachers for work in the Paris Evangelical Missionary Society. A Theological School was later established in 1882 and there are currently ten students.

The Roman Catholic Church is training priests and ministers at Saint Augustine's Seminary. There were 121 men in training in 1987. In addition the Catholic Church has three minor seminaries.

Clergy for the Anglican Church are trained at the National University of Lesotho.

Assembly Bible College in Maseru is a ministry of the Assemblies of God Lesotho. In addition to training ministers for their own denomination, it is being used by other evangelical groups. In 1987 it had thirty students. The Full Gospel Church of God operates a Bible School at Butha Buthe, and the Church of the Bible Covenant has a small training center in Maseru.

The National Baptist Church has a seminary at Leribe.

The Lesotho Bible Training Institute in Maseru trains through correspondence courses. Discipleship training courses are being used by parachurch groups such as Campus Crusade, Global Evangelism Ministries, Youth with a Mission and Scripture Union.

Social concerns

Social activity has been the method of reaching Lesotho with the gospel. The Paris Evangelical Missionary Society (now LEC) commenced schools at each of its mission stations and outstations as they opened and the Roman Catholics followed the same pattern. By 1981 primary school enrollment was as follows:

Roman Catholic Church	111,918
Lesotho Evangelical Church	103,083
Anglican Church in Lesotho	35,007
Government	3,831
Other churches	2,825
Government	2,382

The government is now exercising greater control over primary schools but secondary schools and high schools remain the care of the church.

Churches continue to play a vital role in the health care system of the government. In 1981, 20% of the 114 doctors in the country worked in mission hospitals or clinics while 33% of all outpatients seen were at mission hospitals and clinics.

The Church is deeply involved in relief and development through church agencies such as Catholic Relief Services and Caritas Lesotho in the Catholic Church. Sodepax operates through the Christian Council. Network of Love, a grouping of eighteen church and parachurch agencies, has been involved in an integrated famine relief, church planting and development programs for Lesotho.

NEEDS IN LESOTHO

Lesotho is a Christian country and there is little need for church planting. However there is much nominalism and the church lacks Bible teaching and trained pastors. The primary need then, is for the training of leaders and lay people who will reach out to disciple the nation. Skilled expatriates, prepared to play a servant-role in national churches and emerging indigenous mission groups, could be used for this task. Refresher courses for ministers and pastor's conferences would also be helpful.

Given the high literacy rate, and the eagerness of the people to obtain reading material, greater use could be made of literature for evangelism.

Greater emphasis should be placed on reaching the young people. Religious instruction in secondary schools is almost non-existent because of a lack of trained personnel. This could be an area of increased involvement.

Use of gospel films in villages could be expanded. The Jesus Film, which has been translated into Sesotho, could be a vital evangelistic tool. The limited use of this medium has been enthusiastically received.

Training in stewardship is needed so that pastors and evangelists can be fully employed in the work to which they are called.

The country's social needs are great but great caution needs to be exercised to avoid aid dependency. Programs which encourage self-help and job creation are needed. Training in environmental awareness would prevent the overstocking of the land and serious soil erosion problems. More effective methods of cultivation of crops would assist subsistence farmers to be more productive.

BIBLIOGRAPHY

Annual Statistical Bulletin 1982, Bureau of Statistics, Lesotho

Barrett, David, *World Christian Encyclopedia*

Brading, Barbara and Richard, *Basotholand: Portrait of a Protectorate*, Society for the Propagation of the Gospel

Catholic Directory 1985/86

Central Bank of Lesotho Quarterly Review, December 1986

Cronje, D.R.J.M., *Born to Witness*, NG Kerk Boekhandel

Ellenberger, V., *Landmarks in the Story of the French Protestant Church in Basotholand*

Encounter the New Lesotho, Speeches of King Moshoeshoe II and others, Ministry of Information and Broadcasting

Lesotho Survey, Africa Inland Mission

Mohapeloa, J.M., *From Mission to Church*, Morija

Thorpe, Cyprian, *The Great Queen's Blanket*, SSM

United Bible Societies Bulletin

Wilkinson, Edgar C., *Methodism in Basotholand*, Methodist Mission Department

Woodward, Calvin, "Not a complete solution: Assessing the long years of foreign aid to Lesotho", *Africa Insight Bulletin* No. 3, 1982

CHAPTER THREE

Namibia:

Era of New Opportunities

NAMIBIA

Profile

Natural features: Land area: 842,269 km^2 (318,261 sq miles). Namibia is a vast and largely arid country on the Atlantic seaboard of the southwestern portion of Africa.

Terrain: One-fifth of the total area consists of the barren Namib Desert which stretches between 80 and 120 km along the coastline.

Climate: Rainfall varies from less than 100 mm in the south to above 400 mm in the north and northeast. Temperatures vary from zero temperatures in winter to above 40^{0}C in summer. Arable land: 1%.

Population: (1986 estimate) 1,180,000. Annual growth rate: 2.9% per annum. Population density: 1.4 persons per km^2.

Ethnic groups: Wambo 49%, White 7%, Damara 7%, Herero 7%, Kavango 9%, Nama 5%, Colored 4%, East Caprivi 4%, San (Basarwa Bushmen) 3%, Rehoboth Baster 2%, Tswanas 1%.

Languages: English and Afrikaans are official languages. German is widely spoken. There are fourteen ethnic languages. The major languages of the Owambo people are Oshindonga or Oshikwanyama. Literacy rate: 35%.

Urbanization: 26%. Windhoek (population 110,000) is the capital. Other towns include Luderitz, Tsumeb, Keetmanshoop, Swapkopmund. The port of Walvis Bay is South African territory.

Government: A coalition of six political parties united to form the Transitional Government of National Unity in 1985. Executive authority is vested in the South African appointed Administrator-General. Judiciary functions independently of South Africa, but appellate division through South African Supreme Court.

Economy: Currency: South African rands. 100 cents = R1. R1 = $0.45 (July 1988). GNP: R2,159 million. GNP per capita: R1,870 (1985). Imports: R1,227 million (1985). Exports: R1,569 million, of which 82% was mineral production. Agriculture as a % of

GDP: 6% (1985). Inflation rate: 13.4% (1986). Growth rate: 3.5% (reversal of decline).

Religion: According to the 1981 Census Report, 93% of the population claims to be Christian. Protestant 65% (mainly Lutherans); Roman Catholic 16%; Anglican 7%; African Independent Church 6%; Traditional 6%.

HISTORICAL BACKGROUND

Namibia was originally occupied by Khoisan people (San and Nama) and the Damara people. By the seventeenth century, Owambo and Herero had migrated to the area. The colonization of Namibia did not begin until the nineteenth century when traders and missionaries heralded a colonial scramble for land. In an agreement between Britain and Germany, Namibia was finally annexed by Germany in 1890.

In 1915, at the request of the allied powers, South Africa forced the Germans to surrender and Namibia was brought under South African control. A legislative assembly elected by whites came into existence in 1926.

After 1948, South Africa introduced a system of administration which entrenched ethnic identities at a local government level. South Africa continued to administer Namibia, based on decisions in its favour at the International Court of Justice 1966, despite United Nations protestations. However, a 1971 decision by the Court of Justice ruled in favour of the United Nations and South Africa's administration was declared illegal. SWAPO (South West African People's Organization), an Owambo-based organization, was declared the sole authentic representative of the people of Namibia, despite the fact that de facto government is under South African control. SWAPO's commitment to a path of scientific socialism is supported by the Marxist regime in Angola. The north of Namibia has become a military zone with South African and Namibian forces resisting the Angolan based SWAPO insurgents. The rural population is caught between the two armies who both demand allegiance, and atrocities from both sides of the warring factions are reported.

Meanwhile, in this fragmented and polarized society, South Africa has been experimenting with political models, the latest of which is a multi-party conference which culminated in the establishment of the present Transitional Government of National Unity in 1985. Since 1980, the border war has moved to southern Angola where Cuban and South African troops are in combat.

Withdrawal of Cuban forces from Angola has become a Namibian settlement issue.

THE PEOPLES OF NAMIBIA

More than 60% of Namibia's population live in the northern part of the country which is relatively well-watered and productive. A further 10% live in Windhoek, leaving the remaining 30% of the population scattered across the vast arid and semi-arid land.

The **Wambo**, comprising 49% of the total population, consists of eight tribes with no common language of communication. In this matrilineal society, 69% of the population is under the age of twenty-five years. Some 70% of the Wambo population are Lutheran. Only 3% of the population do not claim allegiance to a Christian church.

The **Kavango** people are divided into five distinct tribal groups. They live along river banks and subsist on fishing, agriculture and cattle-raising. Their society is matrilineal. The majority of these people claim to be Roman Catholic (57%) but a large degree of syncretism exists. Of the remainder, a further 21% claim to have no religion, indicating a strong traditional base.

The **Damara** people, who constitute 7% of the population, are Negroid people culturally aligned to the Khoi (Hottentot) group. They are staunchly Lutheran by tradition.

The **Herero** people, consisting of seven sub-groups, were traditionally nomadic people and are scattered across Namibia. Their revolt against German occupation in 1905 resulted in a genocide which wiped out 80% of the Herero population.

Other ethnic groups are the Nama, Caprivi (two tribes plus sub-groups), Tswana, coloreds, Rehoboth Basters, San, (five groups) and whites, a diminishing population.

Some 30,000 refugees have crossed the border to Namibia to escape the fighting in Angola, resulting in a strong Portuguese element in the northern area.

SOCIO-ECONOMIC CONDITIONS

Namibia has been ethnically divided into ten homelands, each under its own administration on a self-governing basis.

Although discrimination in housing, labor and many other areas has now fallen away, *apartheid* has created wounds which will take many years to heal.

Namibia has a dual economy. The modern sector is based on agriculture and mining, particularly diamonds.

Agriculture

Although agriculture contributed only 6% to the GDP in 1985, it provides employment for more than half of the total labor force. Namibia still looks to South Africa for revenue and in 1987/88, sixteen percent of its budget was funded by South Africa.

As an underdeveloped nation, a priority need in Namibia is the provision of employment opportunities, since subsistence agriculture will not be able to sustain the high population growth rate. Urbanization is increasing rapidly.

Education and health services

Education remains ethnically based and discriminatory. Expenditure on education increased by 32% in the 1986 fiscal year.

Health care has been based in the large centers but the emphasis is changing to preventive health care based at 'bush' clinics with health care workers at the village level. The isolation of rural communities together with the low population density rate makes the task a difficult one.

Table 1: Social Indicators in Brief

Total enrollment in schools (1986)	350,080
Total enrolled in primary schools	77%
Total enrolled in secondary schools	21%
Total enrolled in tertiary education (1986)	1%
Pupil/teacher ratio (1985)	32:1
Number of hospitals (1985)	62
Number of clinics & health posts	158
Population per hospital bed	130
Population per clinic and health post	7,493
Population per doctor (1986)	4,289
Population per nurse (1986)	302
Infant mortality rate (per 1,000 live births)	100

STATUS OF CHRISTIANITY

Namibia is one of the most evangelized countries in Africa and, according to the 1980 census, 93% of the people of the country claim to have some denominational allegiance. For most, however, it is a cultural tie which has developed through contact with a mission school or hospital and does not indicate practising Christians.

Historical review

The first Christian witness to Namibia was in 1805 when the London Missionary Society pioneered the work. They persuaded the Rhenish Mission to enter the field, which they did; then in 1824 the London Missionary Society withdrew, handing over their work to the Rhenish Mission.

In 1868 seven missionaries from the Finnish Missionary Society set sail from Helsinki with the aim of starting a mission in Ovamboland, a destination they would take a year to reach.

These early missionary efforts were discouraging. The first Rhenish missionaries waited twenty years before their message was accepted. For the Finnish missionaries, it was thirteen years before the first convert was made, and the Finnish supporters began to wonder whether it was worth it financially. Other early entrants were the Roman Catholics and Dutch Reformed Church.

The present situation

There is a wide measure of religious freedom. However, the majority of the population live along the northern border in restricted military areas and as a result are highly politicized. For many, their aspirations for political freedom identify them with the Angolan-based SWAPO movement which throws them into conflict with the de-facto government. This is felt in the expulsion of ex-patriate church workers who involve themselves in the political struggle. In the face of continuing uncertainty, both evangelical and ecumenical church groups report growing churches. Organizations working among the youth, such as Scripture Union and Students Christian Movement, report a surge of interest.

Traditional ancestral beliefs are a hindrance to the growth of the Christian church, especially among the Herero and San (Bushmen) tribes.

LESSER REACHED PEOPLES

While the majority of the people of Namibia claim to be Christian, there are people groups who are lesser reached.

The Dutch Reformed Church is working among five language groups of the **San** (Bushmen) people. The first San minister for the Vasekela tribe has been ordained. Congregations for the

Heikum, the Mbarakwena, the Tsumkwe Kung and the Gobabis Kung have been established, but they remain people groups who need to hear the message of salvation. The Maroelaboom Kung, living mainly on farms, are unreached.

The **Herero** people were first evangelized by the Rhenish mission in 1844 and churches were developed. In 1955 they broke away to form a syncretistic Herero church they named Oruuano Church which mingled Christianity with traditional beliefs. Evangelistic ministry has again been commenced. The Himba and Tjimba sub-groups living in Kaokoland are unreached.

The **Hambukushu** tribe which straddles Angola, Namibia and Botswana number about 20,000 in Namibia. Approximately 85% claim to be Roman Catholic, but tribal customs and witchcraft dominate. Until recently there has been no Protestant witness.

NATIONAL CHURCHES

Religious affiliation in Namibia is high as is also church attendance, particularly among the women, but the number of regenerate Christians is low.

The Christian Council of Namibia represents about 80% of Christians. Its members are:

- African Methodist Episcopal Church
- Anglican Church
- Congregational Church
- Evangelical Lutheran Church in SWA/Namibia
- Evangelical Lutheran Church in Namibia
- Methodist Church
- Roman Catholics

The Evangelical Fellowship of SWA/Namibia has recently been established to provide a framework for unity and cooperation. A milestone was reached with the commencement of this body since it is the beginning of inter-denominational as well as cross-cultural cooperation among evangelicals.

Table 2: Religious Affiliation in Namibia

Protestant	65% (includes nominals)
Roman Catholics	16%
Anglican	7%
African Independent Church	6%
Traditional	6%

Evangelicals are estimated to number 10% of the population. The larger denominations are summarized in Table 3.

Table 3: Denominational Membership in Namibia

Evangelical Lutheran Church in Namibia	316,000
Evangelical Lutheran Church in SWA/Namibia	200,000
Roman Catholics	188,000
Anglican Church	80,000
Dutch Reformed Churches	56,000
Seventh Day Adventists	19,000
Rhenish Church in SWA	15,000
Owambo Independent Church	13,000
German Evangelical Lutheran	10,000
African Methodist Episcopal Church	10,600
Rhenish Evangelical Lutheran Church	4,000
Gereformeerde Kerk	3,600
Congregational Church	3,600
Methodist Church	3,200
Church of God World Missions (Full Gospel)	3,000

Roman Catholics

The Roman Catholic Church in Namibia consists of two independent Vicariates. The Vicariate of Keetmanshoop was begun by the saintly pioneer Right Reverend John Simon in 1898. In 1909 it became an independent Prefecture and in 1949 a Vicariate. It has a Catholic population of 26,000.

The Vicariate of Windhoek was originally part of Angola where work began in 1896. It became a Prefecture in 1921 and a Vicariate in 1926. It has a Catholic population of 162,430.

There is a total of forty-five convents and three orders of religious brothers. The Catholic church is responsible for thirty-six churches and twelve hospitals, one of which has recently been taken over by the government. There are fifty-two congregations cared for by sixty-one priests. The first black priest (Tswana) was ordained in 1942.

According to church statistics, Roman Catholics number 188,430 (16% of population) but the 1980 census yields a figure of 204,000 (20%). This compares with 18% of the population in the 1970 census.

Anglican Church

Anglican work commenced in 1924 when Father Tobias established Saint Mary's Mission at Odibo in Ovamboland, and this mission became the center from which other missions were established.

Approximately 85% of church membership is in Ovamboland where military activity is part of life. The Anglican church, however, has suffered heavy war damage which has completely destroyed some of their stations while others have had to be abandoned. Three of their Bishops as well as a Vicar-General have been deported and applications for visas for a number of other workers have been refused. Inevitably the church perceives this harassment to be a lack of religious freedom. Bishop James Kauluma, an Owambo, is an outspoken critic of the present rule.

The church has embarked on a "Partnership in Mission" program which aims to develop people and resources through training in evangelism, relationships, and issues which affect the people in daily life.

The Diocese of Namibia has 120 congregations and an estimated 80,000 members. This compares with 52,000 recorded in the 1980 census. According to these figures, growth has remained at a constant level when compared with population growth rates.

Protestant churches

Lutherans

The Lutheran Church, consisting of three church groups, is the largest denomination in Namibia.

Evangelical Lutheran Church in Namibia (formerly Evangelical Lutheran Owambokavango Church) is the largest church with 316,000 members. The work, started in 1870 by the Finnish Mission, was handed over to national leadership in 1954. Today there are more than sixty parishes served by 110 pastors and 220 evangelists and deacons.

The church emphasizes a gospel which is holistic, ministering in the areas of justice and reconciliation, education and medical work. The Lutheran Medical Mission administers twelve hospitals and twenty-one clinics. The Kavango Bible School gives instruction in Biblical Studies while pastors and theologians are trained at Paulinum United Theological Seminary.

Evangelical Lutheran Church in SWA (Rheinish Mission Church) is the offspring of the missionary endeavors of the Rheinish Mission

Society of Germany. Early missionary efforts which commenced in 1830 were discouraging. Twenty years of ministry elapsed before those early pioneers saw fruit for their labors. Work was established in the central and southern parts of the country and subsequent growth was rapid. Today the church has 200,000 members worshipping in forty-nine parishes.

Leadership was handed over to the indigenous people in 1968 and in 1972 the first black *Prases* was elected head of the church. The church continues to have close ties with its European partners through the United Evangelical Mission.

There is a strong emphasis on education. The church has involvement in twenty boarding schools, twenty preschool centers and a high school. Young women are trained at the Heinz-Stover Institution for hostel and preschool work, a lay training center operates at Berseba, and there is joint participation in the United Theological Seminary.

The *Duitse Evangeliese Lutherse Kerk* serves the German-speaking community. The 1980 census indicates 10,000 affiliates.

According to census reports, the Lutheran churches have grown from 39% of the total population in 1970 to 49% in 1980.

Dutch Reformed Church

The Dutch Reformed family of churches has 56,000 members.

The white *Nederduitse Gereformeerde Kerk* established its first congregation at Mariental in 1891. Its membership reached 60,000 in 1978, but the church is now on the decline as its Afrikaans members leave the territory. It is estimated that membership is now in the region of 20,000.

The first mission outreach was in 1955 to Kaokoland, but since that time a number of mission churches have been established, including:

- Conference of Bushman Congregations
- The Evangelical Reformed Church in Africa
- Evangelical Reformed Church in Owambo
- Igrega Reformada (Angolan refugees)
- Reformed Church in Caprivi

African Independent Churches

It is estimated that there are 100 Independent Churches which comprise 6.5% of the population. This figure includes the Oruuana Church of the Herero people.

CHRISTIAN ACTIVITIES

Evangelism

In a time of social upheaval, there are many who are hungry for the living water that only God can supply, and a number of agencies are seeking to meet these needs. There are churches and missions who feel that God is beginning to revive His Church in Namibia.

Scripture Union is operating in many schools throughout the country and young people are responding to the gospel. Other youth movements include Students' Christian Movement and Namibian National Students Organisation.

Youth with a Mission (YWAM) is challenged with the needs of the Damara people. YWAMers are teaching in government schools as tentmakers. Further opportunities exist in the fields of education and health care.

Africa Evangelistic Band has white and colored workers who conduct missions across the country. Converts are fed into local churches.

Apostolic Faith Mission has conducted rallies in different areas of the country. Many thousands have indicated a desire to follow Christ.

An annual conference under the banner of *ICHTHUS* is being held in Windhoek which aims to win people for Christ, then disciple them through seminars.

Radio Ministry is challenging people to new life in Christ and evangelical streams are developing in ecumenical churches as a result.

Literature

The early Finnish missionaries saw the need for Christian literature and established a printing press in 1903. It was taken over by the Evangelical Lutheran Church in Namibia when the church was nationalized. Situated in the war zone, it was destroyed in 1981 but has subsequently been replaced. It prints books, booklets, pamphlets and magazines in local languages for parish use.

The Evangelical Lutheran Church in SWA/Namibia has a printing press in Karabib and the Roman Catholic Angelus Press is situated in Windhoek.

Windhoek has three Christian bookshops. Christian Mobile Literature, which operates one of these shops, have book outlets in fourteen towns throughout the country. Scripture Union Bible-reading notes are available from the Windhoek office. Youth with a Mission has a large bookshop.

There is a need for Christian literature in the African languages which will challenge the peoples of Namibia to a deeper commitment and daily walk with God.

Bible translation and distribution

The Bible is available in English, Afrikaans, German, Ndonga, Kwanyama, Nama, Portuguese, Tswana, Kwangali and Herero. Portions are available in Mbukushu, Tsumkwe-Kung, Akhoe, Gciriku. Translation work is in progress in a number of these languages. In 1986, 25,700 Bibles, 2,829 New Testaments and 3,574 Scripture portions were sold.

Portions of Scripture have been published in Braille in the Kwanyama language. Translation needs include material in the Mbarakwena language.

Christian education

Paulinum United Lutheran Theological Seminary serves the Lutheran Churches. It offers a four-year pastoral certificate, a Diploma in theology, and a Bachelor of Theology degree. The Engela Parish Institute trains deacons and evangelists for the Evangelical Lutheran Church in Namibia.

The Roman Catholics operate a lay-training center at Gobabis.

It is only recently that evangelicals have become involved in training and the institutions they have established will meet a real felt need.

Windhoek Theological Seminaryopened in 1988 for the training of part-time ministers, lay preachers and church leaders of the evangelical reformed tradition.

Africa Evangelical Fellowship commenced a post-matric training college in Windhoek in 1985, naming it WEBCOR. They are also planning a Bible School at Rundu in the north.

The Full Gospel Church of God has a Bible School at Okavango.

The Southern Baptists offer Bibleway correspondence courses.

Media

SWA Broadcasting Corporation, the local government radio and television service, broadcasts sixty hours of Christian programs a week. These programs, prepared by Christian denominations as well as the staff of the radio service, are evangelical in content and reports are received of many finding new life in Christ.

In some churches, the term "conversion" has become a source of contention as church members, who have heard gospel messages on the radio seek to find the way of salvation within their own denominations. It is resulting in an evangelical stream within the large ecumenical churches.

Radio Owambo is reaching across borders into Angola and reports of people turning to Christ are being received.

Trans World Radio beams programs into Namibia, but surveys indicate that signals are weak and the national service is used in preference.

Media for Christ has an extensive media ministry which includes: Club 700, operating as a subscription Christian video club, reaching up to 15,000 people; Bible teaching videos available for purchase; programs prepared for transmission on SWATV; and a closed-circuit radio ministry operating throughout the country's prisons with a speaker in each cell. The Jesus Film has been translated into a Wambo language and a translation in the Damara-Nama language is in progress. These ministries are resulting in changed lives countrywide.

Social action

The churches in Namibia are deeply involved in social action. The Lutheran Medical Mission under the supervision of the Evangelical Lutheran Church in Namibia (ELCIN) is running a widespread health service. There are twelve hospitals and twenty-one clinics run by four doctors and a nursing staff of 600. Nurses and midwives are trained at Onandjokwe Lutheran Hospital. ELCIN also operates elementary schools at more than sixty centers.

The Roman Catholic church operates eleven hospitals. Saint Antonius Hospital was recently closed when the government refused to renew work permits for Dutch medical staff. Thirty-six schools operate under the Catholic church as well as hostels for school children, preschool facilities and creches.

The Evangelical Lutheran Church in SWA manages twenty hostels for school children and provides preschool education at twenty centers.

Justice and reconciliation

Issues of justice and reconciliation play an important role in the life of the church.

For the ecumenicals, the Christian Council of Namibia serves as a unifying body in its efforts to bring about change, and of paramount importance to this body is the introduction of a new social and political order which will be free of discrimination and oppression. The churches feel they have a prophetic role in speaking against social ills.

At the World Council of Churches conference held in Zambia, its position statement included the following:

> "We affirm the unquestionable right of the people of Namibia to secure justice and peace through liberation movements. While remaining committed to peaceful change we recognize that the nature of the South African regime compels the movements to the use of force along with other means, to end oppression."

The evangelical churches, who for long have remained silent on issues of justice and reconciliation, are making efforts to reach out cross-culturally, and in recent days, God has been at work in the hearts of many. However, in the white community the roots of formalism and superiority are deep and difficult to uproot, and to many in other ethnic groups, their efforts are seen to be paternalistic. There is a new realization that only God can bring about the necessary changes in attitudes among the people of all races.

NEEDS IN NAMIBIA

Namibia is a polarized country with many causes fighting for the hearts and minds of the people. Christ is the only answer to this country's deep problems. There is a need for a clear presentation of Christ's redeeming power.

The churches are polarized with deep divisions between the ecumenical and evangelical camps. Pray that evidences of improving relationships between religious and ethnic groups will continue to grow.

Christian literature in the African languages is a real need. Although there are bookshops and book outlets throughout Namibia, few are situated in areas aimed at reaching indigenous people.

Leadership training in areas of the deeper Christian life and management skills is needed for pastors and lay workers. Advanced training to enable nationals to be involved in the training process is seen to be a need in the evangelical camp.

Tentmakers, both national and expatriate, could make a contribution to the Kingdom of God in government, education and health systems.

Farmworkers in isolated areas (particularly San) are relatively unreached.

BIBLIOGRAPHY

Africa Insight, "South West Africa (Namibia)", Vol. 17 No. 1, 1987

Barrett, David, *World Christian Encyclopedia*, Oxford

Cronje, J.M., *Born to Witness*, NG Kerkboekhandel

Department of Statistics, Pretoria, 1970 & 1960 Census Reports

Department of Statistics, Windhoek, 1980 Census Reports

Europa Publications, *Africa South of the Sahara*

Information Service Windhoek, *Facts and Figures 1987*

Malan, J.S., *Africa Insight*, Vol. 12, No. 3, 1982

CHAPTER FOUR

Republic of South Africa:

Need of Reconciliation

REPUBLIC OF SOUTH AFRICA

Profile

Natural Features: 1,123,226 km^2 (433,678 sq miles) of land area excluding the independent countries within South Africa of Transkei, Bophuthatswana, Venda and Ciskei (TBVC), and including the enclave of Walvis Bay.

Terrain: Two major zones include the interior plateau and the coastal zone, divided by mountain ranges. The interior plateau has an average altitude of 1,200 meters. Altitudes on the escarpment rise to 3,482 meters.

Climate: Rainfall varies from over 1,000 mm a year on the east coast to less than 60 mm a year on the west coast. Average annual rainfall for the country is 464 mm. Some 65% of the country receives less than 500 mm a year. South Africa is prone to cyclical droughts. Annual average temperature is 23°C (12.5°C on the mountain ranges), but temperatures range from 48°C in the northwest to -12°C in the mountains.

Population: (1986 estimate) Total excluding TBVC: 28.4 million, Total including TBVC: 34.3 million. Blacks: 19.6 million; Whites: 4.9 million; Coloreds: 2.9 million; Asians: 893,100. Population density is 100 people per km^2 in the east where the rainfall is high, to less than one person per km^2 in the arid west. Total population density is 25.2 per km^2. Annual growth rate overall is 2.6%: Blacks 2.91%, Coloreds 2.87%, Asians 1.9%, and Whites 1.6%. Children in the 0-14 age group amount to 34% of total population.

Ethnic groups: (1985) Whites (17.2% of the population); Coloreds (10.4%); Asians (3.1%); Blacks (69%) include Zulus (35%), Xhosa (14%), Tswana (8%), North Sotho (14%), South Sotho (11%), Tsonga/Shangaan (6%), Swazi (5%), Ndebele (4%), Venda (1%).

Languages and Literacy: Official languages are Afrikaans and English. Other languages spoken include Zulu, Xhosa, North and South Sotho, Tswana, Luvenda, Shangaan, Siswati, Ndebele, Portuguese and German. Literacy rate is 64% overall: Whites 87%, Asians 78%, Colored 69%, Blacks 51%.

Urbanization: 56% of the total population live in cities and towns: 93% of Asians, 89% of Whites, 78% of Coloreds, and 40% of

Blacks. Pretoria is the capital city (population 849,000 according to 1980 census). Other major cities are Greater Johannesburg (3.46 million), Greater Cape Town (1.7 million), and Greater Durban (1.5 million).

Government: Constitution provides for a State President, a tricameral parliament (whites, coloreds and Asians), a cabinet headed by the State President, and a Ministers Council for each of the three Houses of Parliament. Blacks are excluded from central government. There are ten ethnic black homelands, four of which are independent and six self-governing.

Economy: Currency: 100 cents = 1 Rand; $0.45 = R1 (July 1988). GDP: (1985) R109,604 million. GDP per capita: R3,165. Inflation rate: 14.8% (1987). Contribution to GDP: mining 21%, manufacturing 19%, agriculture 6%. Exports: (1987) R42,717 million. Imports: R28,736 million.

Religion: (Census report 1980) Protestant 41.5%, African Independent Churches 21%, Traditional 15%, Roman Catholic 10%, Anglican 6%, Non-Religious 2.5%, Hindu 2%, Muslim 1.5%.

HISTORICAL BACKGROUND

The original inhabitants of the country were the San (Bushmen or Basarwa) and the Khoi (Hottentots). The first white settlement was in 1652 when Jan van Riebeeck was sent by the Dutch East India Company to establish a halfway house for supplies for their ships. The settlement at the Cape in the southwestern corner gradually moved northward and eastward and the San retreated into the interior. In 1779 the first contact was made in the southeast with blacks who had migrated southward over the centuries from Central Africa, and this was the beginning of years of conflict.

At the end of the 18th century, the Dutch surrendered to British forces, as part of the European conflict. Dutch resentment at British control gave rise to the "Great Trek" in 1835 during which most of the Dutch inhabitants migrated northward, resulting in white occupation of the interior.

In 1910, the four independent colonies which had come into being united to form the Union of South Africa, a self-governing dominion within the British Empire. In 1948 the Afrikaner-based National Party was elected to govern the country by the white electorate, a mandate which it still retains. From 1949 onwards legislation was introduced to implement the policy of separate development (*apartheid*). In 1960 South Africa became a republic and in 1961 it withdrew from the British Commonwealth.

Present government

In 1978 P.W. Botha became Prime Minister, and in 1984, President. New political initiatives were introduced, resulting in bitter opposition from both right-wing Afrikaners and the black population. The introduction of a racially segregated three-chamber parliament brought coloreds and Asians into the parliamentary system, the first time in the history of the country that people other than whites had a place in central government.

President Botha is currently exploring new models of government. Plans have been announced for a new policy-making body comprising leaders of the different communities with a partly elected executive. Meanwhile the general election of 1987 brought about a new political era in white voting support. The National Party, which has been in power for forty years, has liberalized its policies to the extent that it no longer represents the aspirations of the Afrikaners, and there has been a considerable movement to the right-wing Conservative Party.

Black response to the exclusion from political reform has been the formation of extra-parliamentary political groupings which include the United Democratic Front and the Azanian People's Organization. Black trade unions have also become involved in politics. Disillusioned with a professedly capitalistic society, they advocate socialism. With black youths spearheading resistance, a period of intense unrest has followed the 1987 election. Action by township militants resulting in violence and counter-violence led to the view that black resistance was unstoppable and that a new era would soon result in a more just socialist society.

Government powers were unleashed with the proclamation of a State of Emergency giving the police sweeping powers. Press controls and the banning of resistance organizations has followed, and although unrest has largely been controlled, it is accompanied by deep resentment. A likely scenario is low-level violence which could continue for many years.

In response to resistance and despite emergency controls, there has been an apparent retreat from *apartheid* as some legislation has been repealed or amended. *Apartheid* is also crumbling as discrimination becomes less enforceable. Discriminatory laws still remaining in the statute books include the Group Areas Act, the Population Registration Act and the Separate Amenities Act.

The ruling National Party has not emerged unscathed. Afrikaner unity has deep cleavages and a reversion to right-wing politics is possibly a greater threat at this stage than a revolutionary takeover.

A number of government initiatives have been introduced to accommodate the political aspirations of the black population living outside the homelands, none of which have been accepted by this large segment of the population.

Development of the homelands

The tribal authorities operating in the homelands were gradually given greater powers by the ruling National Party until they were eventually superseded by partly tribal, partly Western forms of government. These areas are termed Independent States and National States.

Transkei was the first of these homelands to gain independence[1] (1976) followed by Bophuthatswana (1977), Venda (1979), and Ciskei (1981). Some 53% of the black population of South Africa live in the six National States, while the remaining 47% live permanently in what has traditionally been regarded as "white" South Africa.

PEOPLES OF SOUTH AFRICA

The early inhabitants of South Africa were the **Khoi** (Hottentots) and the **San** (Bushmen). The San, who are hunter-gatherer people, retreated in the face of the new settlement while the Khoi intermarried and became part of the colored population.

Afrikaners comprise about 56% of the white population. They find their origins in early Dutch, German and French Huguenot settlers. Afrikaans was only established as a language in the latter part of the nineteenth century. The Afrikaners are generally conservative religious people of whom 70% are now urbanized. The unity they have known as a people has been shattered by political tensions, resulting in the formation of a conservative grouping (*verkrampte*), and a more enlightened group in favour of political reforms (*verligte*).

---

1   The use of the word independence, Independent or National States does not imply support of such labels or of the system that has generated them.

English settlement began with British occupation in the eighteenth century, but the present English speakers include people from many countries who have adopted English as their home language. The majority of English-speaking peoples live in the cities and comprise 38% of the total white population.

Coloreds are a group of mixed ethnic descent. They include descendants of indigenous peoples and white settlers. Six percent of this group are of Malay descent and staunchly Muslim. The majority are Afrikaans speaking and live in the cities, particularly around Cape Town.

Asians are comprised of Indians (99%) and Chinese (1%). The first group of Indians arrived in 1860 as indentured labor and were followed by independent traders. The majority of these people are of the Hindu faith (64%), while 20% are Muslim. The remainder are Christian. The Hindu group are being effectively evangelized by the Full Gospel Church of God. The majority of Indians are English speaking (73%) and urbanized. Approximately 6% of the Chinese population adhere to Confucianism.

Portuguese number approximately 600,000.

The **black** population can be divided into four main groups: Nguni, Sotho, Tsonga/Shangaan and Venda (see Table 1).

Table 1:   Black People Groups of South Africa

	% of black population	Sub-groups	% of black population
Nguni	58%	Zulu	34.9%
		Xhosa	14.2%
		Swazi	5.2%
		Ndebele	4.0%
Sotho	33%	North Sotho	14.4%
		South Sotho	10.6%
		Tswana	8.3%
Tsonga/Shangaan	6%		
Venda	1%		
Other ethnic groups	1.4%		

Source: Census 1985

SOCIOECONOMIC CHARACTERISTICS

Early economic activity was based on agriculture, but the discovery of minerals in the late nineteenth century changed this picture significantly. Subsequent industrial growth brought this country to what it is today, that of a modern diversified Western economy. With economic development confined mainly to urban areas, a dualistic economy developed, resulting in a rural population which was largely dependent on subsistence agriculture. However, pressure of land and increasing urbanization, an emphasis on black education, and the migrant labor system, has changed the economy of the traditional homestead from a subsistence to a cash economy base.

Education in South Africa is ethnically fragmented. There are eighteen education departments within South Africa and a further ten in the Independent and National States. There is also inequality in the distribution of available funds, with the result that more is spent per capita on a white child than a black child. The amount spent on each child in 1982/83 was R1,385 for whites, R871 for Asians, R593 for coloreds and R196 for blacks.

Missionaries were the first to attempt to educate the black population and until 1954 missions and churches played a significant role in the system. This changed when the government took control of the education system resulting in the provision of schooling for a larger proportion of the population. In 1984, 77% of black children of school-going age were at school, compared to 36% in 1950. However, government control also resulted in the introduction of Afrikaner nationalism into the education system, and it was this factor which initiated the Soweto riots of 1976.

A number of private schools throughout the country have challenged the racist education system and accepted black scholars. A new era in education has commenced with the introduction of multiracial Christian schools, the majority of which have been started by new charismatic groups. There are currently about seventy of these schools throughout the country.

Health care is available at Provincial hospitals while State Health provides community health services. The emphasis of health care is gradually moving from the traditional curative based medicine to preventative health care. Health care in black areas, much of which was pioneered by mission hospitals, has been handed over to the governments of the National States.

Medical Aid societies, partially subsidised by employers, provide private sector medical care for most white families.

South African Traditional Healer's Association (SATHA), has about 180,000 members but it is estimated that there are a further 1.3 million full time or part time healers south of the Limpopo River.

Table 2: Social Indicators

	Total RSA+	White	Colored	Asian	Black
Total enrollment in education (1986)	6,628,637	1,271,593	832,763	257,965	4,266,316
% enrollment in primary schools	64%	39%	64%	49%	72%
% enrollment in secondary schools	30%	42%	32%	41%	26%
% enrollment in tertiary education	5%	18%	3%	9%	1.5%
Pupil/teacher ratio	32:1	19:1	26:1	23:1	41:1
Literacy rate (1980)	64%	87%	69%	78%	51%
Population per hospital bed*	796				
Population per physician*	476				
Population per nurse	654	271	621	845	1,078
Infant mortality rate per 1000 (1983)	55	13	55	20	80
0-14 age group (1985)	34%	26%	35%	33%	37%
65 age group (1985)	4.7%	8%	3%	3%	4%

* Non-governmental medical services are integrated and an accurate ethnic breakdown is not possible.

+ These statistics exclude Independent and National States. Statistics for the homelands can be found in Addenda 2 and 3. Comparative statistics for other South African countries can be found in Addendum 1.

STATUS OF CHRISTIANITY

Early Church and mission history

Bartholomew Dias, an early Portuguese navigator, landed at Santa Cruz Island in Algoa Bay in 1486 and established the first Christian symbol when he erected a cross. Following soon after,

Vasco da Gama raised a cross at Mossel Bay. A small chapel was built in 1501 which became the first place of Christian worship in South Africa. But these early Roman Catholic beginnings did not result in an established work. In fact the early settlement at the Cape was staunchly Protestant and no Catholic worship was permitted until 1804 when an ordinance allowing for freedom of religion was issued. This forbearance was short-lived. Only two years later the Catholic priests were ordered out of the country. It was not until 1838 that a resident Catholic bishop arrived and he soon established missions across the Cape.

The earliest established church was the Dutch Reformed Church. Colonial settlement commenced in 1652. The first resident minister was Joan van Arckel, who arrived at the Cape with the mandate to care for the spiritual needs of the Dutch settlers.

The Church of England was the first of the English speaking churches. Services began in 1749 in Cape Town.

Ministry to the indigenous people commenced early in colonial history. The Dutch felt a responsibility to their subjects and by 1681 over a thousand slave children and forty adults had been baptized. George Schmidt, a Moravian, arrived in Cape Town in 1736 with the specific responsibility of reaching the Khoi (Hottentot) people. He founded a station at Baviaan's Kloof but met with opposition due to the fact that he was not ordained. Sadly he was recalled, but he left behind a nucleus of believers. Fifty years were to elapse before the Moravians attempted a new missionary enterprise, and on their arrival they were overjoyed to find an eighty-two-year-old woman who had kept her faith.

The London Missionary Society was an early entrant to the country. In 1799 Doctor van der Kemp arrived at the Cape and together with other workers established mission stations in the eastern frontier and in the northern Cape.

The Dutch Reformed Church continued to grow in numbers and in power and today it remains the largest denomination. Schisms, however, developed in the mid-nineteenth century. The Dutch, who had trekked to the interior to escape British domination, established their own churches and eventually many of these new churches separated to form the Nederduitsch Hervormde Kerk. A further breakaway occurred when a number of churches resisted what they felt to be liberalization of the mother church. These churches, mainly rural, grouped to form the Gereformeerde Kerk.

Other churches which have played an important role in the early history of missions are the Methodist Church, started in 1816 by Barnabas Shaw, and the Lutheran churches, the first of which was established in Cape Town in 1780.

The Church today

South Africa is a professedly Christian country with freedom of religion. The 1980 census statistics indicate that 77% of the population is Christian. The Constitution of the country supports this position when it talks of being in "submission to Almighty God who controls the destinies of nations and the histories of peoples." There is prayer and religious instruction in schools, and time is given on national radio and television for religious services. There is, however, a large degree of nominalism in the churches.

South Africa is a hurting country and this is reflected in the condition of the church. Deep divisions are based on differing expectations from the government and its policies. Perspectives differ widely on socialism versus capitalism and in social and political justice alongside theology of liberation. An unwillingness persists on the part of white South Africans to realize a new social era has dawned; and there is a policy of non-involvement in politics by evangelical fundamentalists.

The polarization within the Christian church arises from the history of the country's development and the role the church has played in its progress and policy-making. It is not surprising then, that attempts to find solutions to these problems are being worked out in the church. The black population, denied a platform in the political arena, has found acceptance and recognition in mainline ecumenical churches and is using its voice to bring about reform in its struggle for social and political justice. The tension has been exacerbated by restrictions placed on political organizations by the government. Conservative Afrikaners are also using the church, but to maintain the *status quo*. The black community, particularly the youth, are becoming disillusioned with Christianity. Commitment to Christ is consequently being replaced by commitment to political organizations which offer "freedom."

The politicization of the churches has not been accepted by all. The census reports indicate that people could be "voting with their feet." The ecumenical churches as well as the Afrikaans reformed churches are on the decline. In the black population the move has been to African Independent Churches which are largely apolitical, and in the white and colored community to the Pentecostal and charismatic churches.

The evangelicals, who have largely been silent on issues of justice and socio-political concerns, know that Christ is the only solution to the country's deep needs, and are awakening to the fact that they have a part to play in the unfolding drama.

The church in South Africa has become very nominal. Renewal is needed, particularly in the ecumenical denominations.

Church and State

Both ecumenical and Afrikaans churches have played a political role, particularly since the National Party came to power. In the case of reformed Afrikaner religion, the church has been used to give theological credence to political policies. It is only over the past few years that church leaders are moving away from the philosophy that apartheid could be justified in Scripture. A new policy statement, "Church and Society", issued by the Dutch Reformed Church, states "Racism is a grievous sin which no person may defend or practice." Conservative elements in the church, however, are fighting against integration.

Ecumenical churches feel they have a responsibility to understand and represent social ills, and believe the time has come to demonstrate non-violent resistance. Some go further. The Lusaka Statement[2] states, "We affirm the unquestionable right of the people to secure justice and peace through liberation movements." It further compels the movements to make use of force along with other means to end oppression.

Minister of Law and Order Adriaan Vlok has warned that he will not hesitate to take action against churches which take the road of confrontation, stating that churches are becoming more and more involved in preaching revolution rather than teaching the true Christian message.

Because the overwhelming urgency of the situation is keenly felt by blacks and many whites, there is a determination to involve the church in the solution. The form of action this involvement takes is a matter of interpretation.

---

2   Drawn up by the WCC and accepted by the South African Council of Churches (Excerpt from *Ecunews* August 1987)

South Africa needs the prayers of God's people: that a more just society will result; that there will be reconciliation amongst her peoples; that the nation will turn to Christ who alone can offer peace and salvation from sin.

UNREACHED PEOPLES

More than three centuries have elapsed since Christianity was brought to South Africa yet, although there are few areas where there are no Christian churches, there are still people who need to hear the message of salvation.

Muslims

Muslims in South Africa have not been effectively reached with the gospel. There are three distinct groups:

Indian Muslims number 165,000 (1980 census). They live mainly in the Durban, Johannesburg and Pretoria areas. These hard-to-reach people are very resistant to Christianity and very few have become Christians. The majority (72%) are English speaking.

Colored Muslims live mainly in the Cape and are predominantly of Malay origin. They number 176,000 (1980 census). Missionaries working amongst these people find them less resistant to Christianity. Most of these Muslims are Afrikaans speaking.

Black Muslims number 9,000. This number includes a people group of 1,000 Zanzibarians whose ancestors arrived in this country in 1873 as indentured laborers. They have maintained their Islamic heritage in a distinct community throughout this period.

Hindus

Of the population of 893,000 Asians, 64% are Hindu. The Full Gospel Church of God and the Roman Catholics have made the greatest impact on this community. Small numbers of whites, coloreds and blacks have turned to Hinduism.

Traditionalists

Traditionalists total 15% of the black population, (1980 census). The percentage of people following traditional forms of worship is decreasing according to the census reports. In 1970 the adherence in this category was 27% and in 1960, 32%. Venda, Gazankulu and Lebowa are areas which have the greatest concentration of traditionalists.

Traditional religion acknowledges a supreme being, the creator or original ancestor. The vital part of their religion is the role of the ancestors. Their spirits have power to regulate the life of the living for good or bad and need to be appeased and thanked. This is done through sacrifice of animals or beer. The male head of the family is responsible to the family for maintaining good relationships with the dead. The supreme being is approached through the ancestors.

Mozambique refugees

No accurate figure for the total number of refugees is available but unofficial estimates put the figure as high as half a million people who have fled hardship and atrocities in Mozambique. Many church and mission groups are ministering to the physical and spiritual needs of these unreached people.

Jews total 121,000. Of this figure, 97% are white. There are more than 2,000 Black Jews.

Satanists are estimated to number 100,000.

There are more than 7,000 **Confucians** of whom 83% are black.

NATIONAL CHURCHES

Table 3: Religious Affiliation according to 1980 Census (excluding Independent States)

Protestant	41.5%
African Independent Church	21.0%
Traditional	15.0%
Roman Catholic	10.0%
Anglican	6.0%
No Religion	2.5%
Hindu	2.0%
Islam	1.5%

Andrew Murray, in his survey of missions in 1906, listed thirty-one missionary societies in South Africa. An extensive survey conducted in 1938 under the banner of the Christian Council noted 130 churches, missions and church organizations. Today there are between eighty and 100 denominations and groups of churches operating in South Africa plus 3,000 to 4,000 African Independent Churches.

Although census figures on religious affiliation differ from church membership rolls, they do give an indication of how people feel about their religious beliefs. There appears to be a trend developing away from the mainline denominations. This is particularly true in the white churches. The Roman Catholic and Pentecostal churches have increased their affiliation. A negative factor has been the increase in the number of people who state they have no religion. (See Addendum 4 for ethnic breakdown.)

In the black community the African Independent Churches have increased significantly, at the expense of both mainline churches and traditional religion.

Table 4: Religious Affiliation According to Church Statistics*
(Memberships of more than 10,000, excluding African Independent Churches)

	Church+ Members	# of Churches	# of Ministers
African Methodist Episcopal Church	45,620	120	160
Alliance Church	15,500	302	78
Apostolic Faith Mission in Africa (1987)	64,682	160	314
Apostolic Faith Mission of SA	221,314	1,325	473
Assemblies of God	250,000	1,500	700
Baptist Union of SA (1988)	26,160	238	380
Calvyn Protestante Kerk	20,000	34	24
Christian Brethren		110	
Church of Christ	11,000	162	
Church of the Nazarene (1987)	40,000	729	525
Church of the Province of SA (est)	2,000,000	1,200	1,300
Church of England in SA	20,000	185	79
Evangelical Lutheran Church in SA	558,250	1,464	402
Evangelical Lutheran Church in SA (Natal/Transvaal)	15,000		
Evangelical Presbyterian Church of SA	55,000	40	30
Free Lutheran Church in SA	32,100		
Full Gospel Church of God	130,000	300	430
Gereformeerde Kerk in SA	116,030	291	273
Greek Orthodox Church	60,000	18	
International Fellowship of Christian Churches (1988)	250,000	493	
Methodist Church of SA	596,000	1,822	716
Moravian Church in SA (est)	150,000	67	138
Nederduitsch Hervormde Kerk (1987)	133,000	304	251
Nederduitse Gereformeerde Kerk (1987)	1,426,212	1,193	1,946

	Church Members	# of Churches	# of Ministers
Nederduitse Gereformeerde Kerk in Afrika (1987)	830,029	110	95
Nederduitse Gereformeerde Sendingkerk (1987)	462,436	266	198
Pentecostal Holiness Church	34,000	750	
Pinkster Evangelie Kerk	600,000	300	300
Pinkster Protestante Kerk	12,000	120	130
Presbyterian Church of Africa	231,000		116
Presbyterian Church of SA	75,000	245	256
Reformed Presbyterian Church	50,000	1,000	74
Roman Catholic Church	2,525,660	2,500	1,058
Seventh Day Adventists	20,235	184	122
United Apostolic Faith Church	37,000	360	
United Congregational Church of SA	160,354	225	194

* The statistics include the Independent and National States with the exception of the Methodist Church of SA and the Baptist Union of SA, which do not include Transkei

+1986 unless otherwise stated

It is of interest to note that membership of the combined churches totals about 40% of the census figures, giving indication of a large degree of nominalism in the church. There are an estimated 14,000 ministers in South Africa, one for every 2,200 people.

Although Afrikaners have traditionally been more regular church-attenders than the English community, a survey conducted in 1982 indicated that only 40% of church members attend church regularly. It can be assumed that the active church members in the mainline English churches would be lower.

Coordinating bodies

The South African Council of Churches (SACC) is a powerful organization affiliated to the World Council of Churches. According to church membership, it represents 18% of the total population. It has fifteen member churches and an 80% black affiliation. The SACC is an outspoken critic of the government and its policies.

The Evangelical Fellowship of South Africa, established in 1973, represents seventeen organizations and churches of the evangelical tradition. It is a member of the Association of

Evangelicals of Africa and Madagascar, and the World Evangelical Fellowship.

The South African Catholic Bishop's Conference is the organ through which the Catholic Church in South Africa speaks and acts. Although it is not a member of the SACC, it supports the goals and aims of the organization.

The Council of African Independent Churches, Reformed Independent Churches Association, African Independent Churches Association, and African Spiritual Churches Association are organizations which attempt to bring the many fragmented African Independent churches together.

Table 5: Ratios of Ministers, Churches and Members[3]

Group	Members per Church	Members per Minister	Ministers per Church
Reformed	320	270	0.8
Pentecostal	360	325	0.9
Anglican	1,700	1,700	1.0
Lutheran	1,200	380	0.3
Other Protestants	480	280	0.6
Roman Catholics	2,200	3,200	1.5
OVERALL	680	535	0.8

Roman Catholic Church

The early settlement at the Cape was strongly opposed to Catholicism, but Bishop Griffith's arrival in 1838 heralded a new era. Together with two priests, Bishop Griffith covered vast areas of the Cape by ox-wagon, establishing missions. By the time he died in 1851, the church was established and Catholicism accepted.

The Catholic Church has grown rapidly. In 1916, statistics indicated there were 260 churches and chapels. By 1955 this figure had increased to 1,061. In 1982 further growth had raised this figure to 2,500 churches, caring for a Catholic community of more than 2.5 million. Deep commitment to social action is evidenced in the number of institutions. In 1982 there were 336 church schools, eighty hostels, twenty orphanages, thirty-eight

---

3   Brierley, Peter, *"Church Membership in South Africa"*

hospitals and 150 other institutions including training centers and special schools for the handicapped.

According to the census reports, Catholics numbered 6.7% of the total population in 1960, 8.7% in 1970 and 9.6% in 1980. This church growth is spread across all racial groups.

Anglican Churches

Church of the Province of Southern Africa

Although the first Anglican service was held in Cape Town in 1749, a century was to elapse before Robert Gray was installed as the first Bishop of Cape Town. At that time there were ten Anglican churches. Division arose on doctrinal issues and in 1870 the Church of the Province of Southern Africa was formed with the support of most of the churches.

The Church of the Province of Southern Africa grew rapidly, developing mission stations, hospitals and schools. The church played an important role in black education until the education system was taken over by the state in 1954. This has resulted in a strong black work. The church still involves itself in twelve multiracial private schools and in colored mission schools.

Today there are a total of 1.5 million Anglicans (1980 census), of whom 52% are black. There are seventeen diocese in Southern Africa, of which eleven are in South Africa. A total of 1,300 priests minister at 1,200 churches in the seventeen diocese.

Clergy are trained in three theological colleges.

Church of England in South Africa

After the withdrawal of Robert Gray and his supporters, the Church of England continued under the leadership of Bishop Colenso, but with a diminished following. Several decades of disputes with the Church of the Province followed. Church growth was low. A turning point came in 1955 when the work consolidated and expanded into Zimbabwe and Namibia. The church's estimated membership in South Africa today is 20,000 people (1980 census figures, however, place it at 72,000). The Church of England is governed by a synod and is reformed and evangelical in its theology.

Protestant Churches

Nederduitse Gereformeerde Kerk (Dutch Reformed Church)

The origins of this church date back to 1665 when the first resident minister arrived and established a congregation. Initially the church retained its ties with the mother church in Holland but these ties were broken with the establishment of British colonial government.

As the colonists moved eastward and northward, new congregations were formed. A synod was eventually established in the Cape in 1824 which controlled the churches countrywide, but this changed when the four provinces, which were later to form the Union of South Africa, were established. The Dutch Reformed Church followed the same policy and established separate autonomous churches in each of the provinces. A century was to elapse before these churches were reunited in one general synod. Today there are eleven synods operating on a presbyterian system of church government. The Dutch Reformed Church family is the largest denomination. Its members total 3.6 million, accounting for 12.5% of the total population (census 1980).

In 1824 the church commenced an outreach to the indigenous people and slaves. They worshiped in integrated congregations until 1857 when the Synod reached a decision to commence separate services in separate buildings. This decision resulted in the establishment of a mission church specifically for colored people. In 1881 the **Nederduitse Gereformeerde Sendingkerk** (Dutch Reformed Mission Church) was constituted with four churches and 1,800 members. Current membership is 432,784 (1987). This compares with 675,000 who claimed affiliation in the census report. According to census statistics, the church represented 29% of the colored population in 1960, 28% in 1970, and 25% in 1980. This church is vociferous in its opposition to the racial policies of the mother-church. Its leader, Reverend Allan Boesak, has become a political figure and is a strong advocate of liberation theology.

Mission work to the black population began later; it was not until 1963 that the first general synod of the **Nederduitse Gereformeerde Kerk in Afrika** (Dutch Reformed Church in Africa) was held. This church has 474 congregations with nearly 820,000 members and adherents, and is increasing faster than the population growth rate, according to the census reports. It constitutes 6.5% of the total black population.

Work among the Asian community commenced in 1947. The **Reformed Church in Africa**, which emerged from this work, has ten churches with a total of 2,386 members.

Missionary work by this family of churches was initiated in a number of African countries, all of which are now completely independent of South Africa. They include:

- Church of Christ in the Sudan (Nigeria)
- Dutch Reformed Church in Botswana
- Igreja Reformada em Mocambique
- Nkhoma Synod of the CCAP in Malawi
- Reformed Church in Caprivi
- Reformed Church in Zambia
- Reformed Church in Zimbabwe
- Reformed Church of East Africa (Kenya)

This large church group is deeply involved in serving the country through social action. It operates homes for children and for the aged. Special institutions include schools for the deaf and blind, hostels for unmarried mothers, care centers for alcoholics and drug dependents, and youth centers in urban areas.

Nine ethnically segregated theological seminaries and colleges serve these four South African reformed churches.

The development of separate churches for the different race groups has led many to believe that the policy of apartheid had its origins in the Dutch Reformed Church. The National Party certainly found support for its ideologies in the church which supplied it with the scriptural basis for its policy of racial separation. A new theological stance, however, was accepted at the General Synod of 1986 when it declared, "Racism is a grievous sin which no person or church may defend or practice." The new statement's acceptance as a policy for the church created many tensions and resulted in a breakaway from the mother church to form a new conservative denomination.

Methodist Church of Southern Africa

Reverend Barnabas Shaw arrived at the Cape in 1816. He requested permission to minister to the white community but this was refused. He was also refused permission to work among the colored people. Undeterred, he purchased a wagon and journeyed north where he established a mission in Namaqualand. In 1920, Reverend William Shaw arrived in the Eastern Cape with a group of settlers. After establishing a church among the white community, he carried on to commence a number of mission stations among the Xhosa people.

The work established in those early years was called the Wesleyan Methodist Church of Southern Africa. This was changed to Methodist Church in South Africa in 1931 when three Methodist bodies united, and more recently, the name was changed to the Methodist Church of Southern Africa.

By the turn of the century this church had grown to a membership of 103,000. By 1950 this figure had increased to 470,000 (census 1.3 million). In 1986 the total church membership was 596,000. This compared with 2.2 million who claimed to be Methodists in the 1980 census. Compared with the population growth rate, this denomination is on the decline. As a percentage of the total population, it numbered 10.6% of the population in 1960, 10.5% in 1970 and 8.9% in 1980 (census figures used). According to church statistics, membership amounts to only 2.1% of the total population.

The Methodist church made a great contribution to black education. At the time of the government takeover of schools, they were caring for 170,000 pupils. In addition, they established a number of mission hospitals and operate children's and old-age homes.

Lutheran Churches

A number of Lutheran mission societies played a part in South African church history. The earliest of these was the Berlin mission (1834) which commenced work among the Khoi people and later among the Bapedi. Other Lutheran missions included the Norwegian Mission (1844), the Hermannsburg Missionary Society (1854), and Church of Sweden Mission (1876). The majority of the Lutheran churches united in 1967 to form the Evangelical Lutheran Church in Southern Africa. Their membership numbered 552,000 in 1985. The 1980 census records a figure of 887,000, which includes several smaller church groups as well as autonomous churches. The Lutheran church is declining as a percentage of the total population.

International Fellowship of Christian Churches

The growth of the new charismatic churches has been phenomenal. Commencing with large churches such as Hatfield Christian Church and Rhema, the number of churches has grown to 430 with an estimated membership of 250,000. House churches play an important role in the growth of these groups.

African Independent Churches (AIC)

The rise of the Independent Church movement in South Africa has been dramatic. Today it is the most important religious category amongst black Christians, accounting for 30% of the black population of South Africa in the 1980 census.

This movement had its beginnings in the late nineteenth century when dissident black church leaders moved out of their mainline or mission churches to begin their own groups. By 1913 there were an estimated thirty separatist churches. By 1955 this figure had grown to 1,200 groups. Today there are an estimated 3,000 to 4,000 such churches.

Some of these churches are small and may involve no more than an extended family, while others are very large.

There are two main sub-groups within this movement:

Ethiopian churches are the result of secession from mainline or other independent churches. They have generally retained the doctrinal teaching of their parent bodies, but are very nationalistic in outlook.

The emphasis in *Zionist churches* is the Spirit, revelation, healing and baptism with purification rites. The Spirit and revelation may take precedence over the Scriptures.

The growth of the African Independent churches has been steady over the past three decades. In 1960 there were 2.3 million followers accounting for 21% of the black population. In 1970 this figure had risen to 2.7 million and in 1980, 4.6 million, accounting for 30.1% of the black population. The incidence of church members is evenly spread between urban and rural areas.

The reason for this surge of interest in the indigenous black churches appears to be a rejection of Western-oriented churches which are not meeting felt needs. The AIC churches allow for free expression. Worship, singing, dancing and hand-clapping are forms with which they are familiar.Their small congregations provide a closeness of fellowship and a leadership structure which provides affirmation to people caught between two cultures. Their blend of Christianity is attractive to those who wish to accept Christianity but still adhere to traditional beliefs.

In some groups Jesus Christ is secondary to the Holy Spirit, and at times there is a lack of distinction between the spirits of the ancestors and the Holy Spirit.

The largest of these churches is the Zion Christian Church. The 1980 census records a following of half a million, but the church claims membership of three million.

MISSIONARY SOCIETIES

Early settlers to South Africa were accompanied by clergy who came to serve the needs of the colonists. Most of the churches in the black community, however, have had their origins in foreign missionary societies. The churches formed as a result of these endeavors are now well established national churches which are themselves reaching out into mission.

Nevertheless, a number of missionary societies are currently operating in South Africa. They can be divided into three categories:

Societies with headquarters outside South Africa but working within the country (total of twenty). Included in this group are organizations such as:

- Africa Evangelical Fellowship
- Christian Missions in Many Lands
- The Evangelical Alliance Mission
- Holiness Union Mission
- SIM International
- Southern Baptist Convention
- Swedish Alliance Mission

All of these missions are assisting established national churches.

Societies working in South Africa with local headquarters (total of twenty-seven).

Societies in South Africa for overseas recruitment and fundraising (total of twenty-two).

In addition to the missionary societies noted above, there are a further sixty to eighty parachurch organizations working in the fields of social action, literature distribution, and ministry to youth and children.

Approximately 700 South Africans are working locally as missionaries while no less than 270 are serving overseas.

Missionaries working cross-culturally in South Africa need great wisdom in understanding culture and political tensions.

CHRISTIAN ACTIVITIES

Evangelism

Christ's last injunction to his church to "go into all the world and preach the gospel ... and make disciples," is still as relevant to South Africa in current times as it was two or three centuries ago.

Early missionaries and ministers brought the message of salvation to Southern Africa but much of the credit for the establishment of churches must be given to pioneer African pastors and evangelists who carried the message to distant corners of the country.

Today, there are still those who need to hear the message of salvation and they are to be found in traditional homesteads; among the many nominal Christians who have lost contact with their churches; in urban townships where the youth have rejected Christianity; and in wealthy white homes where materialism has become a god.

In addition to the many churches that run their own evangelism programs, parachurch organizations are conducting mass evangelism campaigns, or they are preaching in small teams. These include:

- Africa Enterprise
- Africa Evangelistic Band
- Christ for All Nations
- Dorothea Mission
- Evangelical Christian Outreach
- Jesus Alive Ministries
- Life Ministry
- Nicky van der Westhuizen Ministries
- Revival Challenge Ministry
- Youth with a Mission

Ministry to students and young people is vital in this troubled land. Youth for Christ and Scripture Union together have committed themselves to reach every secondary school in the country over a three-year period. This vision is called "Youth Harvest". Organizations with campus ministries include Life Ministry, Student Christian Movement, Students' Christian Association, the YMCA and the YWCA. Other movements reaching the youth are Africa Youth Evangelism, who reach black young people through a camping ministry, Baptist Youth with its WOW team, and Youth Alive.

Many other means are being used to reach the nation for Christ including literature, radio and television, social action and development.

Ministry to migrant workers on the mines is an effective way of reaching men from rural areas as well as those from neighboring countries. A number of missions have ministries on the mines, including Christian Ministry to Miners (AEF), while a number of churches have established churches in the area to minister to those of their denomination.

Radio and television

Government-controlled radio and television broadcasts twenty-three radio services in nineteen languages. It also operates four television services in seven languages. Audience research figures show that twelve million adults tune in to the various radio programs. The extensive religious broadcasts on the national service give indication of the interest in religion in South Africa.

In addition to the government services, radio and television broadcasts are transmitted from Bophuthatswana and Lesotho and both these services have religious programs.

Trans World Radio, operating from Swaziland, beams its broadcasts to reach Pedi, Sotho, Tswana, Xhosa, and Zulu language groups, while Radio Pulpit transmits programs over SABC 2000 for forty-six hours a week in English and Afrikaans, as well as Greek, German, Portuguese and Dutch.

There are many agencies involved in the preparation and presentation of these non-governmental programs. They include:

- Africa Evangelical Fellowship
- Baptist International Missions Service
- Church of the Nazarene
- Dorothea Radio Ministry
- Evangeli Xhosa Bible School
- Life Ministry
- MEMA (Dutch Reformed Church)
- Portuguese Radio Ministry
- Radio Evangelisasie SA

Literature

South Africa has a rich heritage of Christian literature. Early missionaries invariably commenced their ministry with the establishment of schools and as the communities became literate, reading material became necessary. Robert Moffat was an early pioneer in Christian literature and printing. He hauled a handprinting press by ox-wagon from Cape Town and for forty years printed Scriptures, books and pamphlets. By the end of the nineteenth century a number of denominations were producing Christian literature, namely Roman Catholics at Marianhill, the American Board Mission, Anglicans, Lutherans and Methodists. One of the most famous church publishing houses was established at Lovedale by the Glasgow Missionary Society.

Today there are many Christian printers and publishers. A total of forty are listed in the *SA Christian Handbook*, the majority of which are denominational. There are, however, a number of large non-denominational printers. All Nations Gospel Publishers, for example, distributes literature to 123 countries. They produce literature in forty Southern African languages. Some 90% of this publisher's production is distributed free. Another large independent publisher is Emmanuel Press at White River which also distributes Christian literature to many parts of the world.

There are approximately 200 Christian bookshops throughout the country. The majority of these are in urban areas and are targeted at the white community. There is a need for the establishment of book depots in rural areas to meet the needs of rural black people.

Scripture translation and distribution

In the early history of South Africa, Bibles were cherished possessions but difficult to obtain, particularly in the interior. Reverend George Thom of the London Missionary Society confirms this in an account of a 1,200 mile trip he made on horseback in 1810. He noted that most of the farmhouses had large unwieldy Bibles handed down from father to son, but that there were no Bibles available when new families were established. One minister rode thirty days' journey to Cape Town in an attempt to acquire Bibles for his congregation.

The first record of formal Bible distribution was in 1806, when the British and Foreign Bible Society sent a consignment of Bibles to the Cape for British soldiers. In 1810, the spiritual needs of the Khoi were considered and a chest of Dutch Bibles and New Testaments arrived for the Moravian and London Missionary Society missionaries. "We cannot find words to express our gratitude," were the words of a Moravian missionary.

Robert Moffat was the first to translate Scripture into an African language. He undertook the translation of the Bible into Tswana and in 1830, the gospel of Luke was published. In 1857 the whole Bible was printed on a hand printing press in Moffat's church at Kuruman. The earliest Xhosa translation was in 1833, and the first Scripture publication in Zulu in 1846. The first Sotho Scriptures were translated by Paris Evangelical Mission workers in what is now Lesotho. An important milestone was reached in 1933 when the first Afrikaans Bible was published.

Today the Bible is available in all the languages of Southern Africa, except Siswati, and new translations and revisions of several languages are in progress. The Bible Society distributes Scripture in 113 languages and, although cutbacks have been necessary because of the country's financial position, thirty-two new publications in ten languages were produced in 1986. Distribution of English, Afrikaans, Zulu and Xhosa accounts for 75% of the total. Sales of different versions of the English Bibles show an interesting trend. Good News Bible accounted for 46% of sales; New International Version, 34%; King James Version, 12%; and Revised Standard Version, 7%. The distribution of Scripture cassettes in indigenous languages has reached encouraging levels. New language translations were Siswati in the New Testament and Psalms (formerly Zulu was used) and Mbukushu.

Scripture circulation in 1987 was 646,350 Bibles, 188,849 New Testaments, 262,652 portions and selections and 20,183 new reader selections. This is a drop from the previous year's figures when sales of 697,350 Bibles, 347,349 New Testaments, 345,360 portions and selections, and 44,577 new readers selections were distributed.

Christian education

In the early history of the church in South Africa, ordained ministers were sent from overseas to minister to both the colonists and the indigenous people. The training of pastors and evangelists was seen as a priority, and much of the credit for the growing churches lay at the hands of dedicated black evangelists. By 1910 there were 703 ordained white ministers and 395 black pastors ministering throughout the country, which gives an indication of the extent of training undertaken. By 1925 these figures had increased to 880 white and 513 black ministers. In 1952 comparable figures were 2,468 white and 928 black ministers. One of the earliest centers for theological training was at Healdtown, where the Methodists commenced training in 1867.

Today there are more than 100 Seminaries, theological colleges and Bible colleges offering full-time study.

In addition there are short-term courses and part-time training institutes, theological education by extension and correspondence courses to assist those who are unable to study full-time.[1]

A new ministry seen especially in the charismatic churches, is the establishment of multiracial Christian schools for children. The American "Accelerated Christian Education" courses are generally being used.

Social action

Education

Schooling for children is where missions began in South Africa. In fact, education came to be associated with missions. In 1854 there were 120 mission schools and by the turn of the century this figure had grown to 1,265. The London Missionary Society at Kuruman was one of the forerunners in establishing schooling for indigenous people. Missions battled to keep these schools going. There was a serious shortage of teachers, and a lack of finances, and facilities were poor. In 1954 the government took over control of all education. With the exception of a few private schools, missions and churches relinquished their control.

Medical care

As mission stations were set up, missionaries became aware of the physical needs of the people. There was much poverty and disease. Doctors and trained nurses established a network of mission hospitals throughout the rural areas of the country. The earliest medical missions were opened by the London Missionary Society, the Church of Scotland and the Anglicans, but later, most churches were involved in providing medical care. By 1970 there were more than 100 mission hospitals. A government commission recommended the provision of a National Health Service and from that time the mission hospitals were gradually placed under government or homeland control.

Social care

Apart from education and medical care, the church is deeply involved in social action. There are fifty-three homes and special

---

1   Courses range from university level to the training of evangelists with a minimum education.

schools for the handicapped, over half of which are run by the Dutch Reformed Church. In addition to these special schools, there are many other training schools being run by churches and Christian organizations to train people in job creation and literacy, not only in rural areas but also in centres operated by urban churches.

There are more than 150 homes for the aged with 10,000 beds. Again the Afrikaans reformed churches are the leaders in caring for the elderly in their churches. The majority of these homes (137) cater to the white community. The 1980 census indicated there was a total of more than a million elderly people of whom one third were white. It is of interest that there are no homes for the aged in the Asian community where it is socially unacceptable for the aged to be cared for outside of the home.

There are eighty-six children's homes run by the churches, caring for more than 7,000 children. The government assists in financing these homes.

The majority of the denominations are involved in relief and development projects, which may vary from soup kitchens to large development schemes. These churches include:

- Apostolic Faith Mission
- Dutch Reformed Church
- Methodist Church of SA
- Presbyterian Church of SA
- Roman Catholics
- Salvation Army
- Seventh Day Adventists

The largest parachurch organization involved in people development is World Vision, which has offices in six centers. Working through 240 projects, its ministries include preschool care, health care, relief feeding and water development.

Other parachurch groups involved in social action include Africa Cooperative Action Trust, Diakonia, Mahyeno Mission, Mfesane, and Africa Enterprise.

INDEPENDENT AND NATIONAL STATES

The development of the homelands is based on the ethnic divisions of the separate groups and is one of the pillars of the policy of separate development (*apartheid*). It aims to give each of the ethnic groups the right to control its own affairs. Although the ideology is racist, Afrikaners argue that they are allowing each race group to maintain its cultural and language identity, a privilege they have fought for in their own culture.

With this policy of partition the government has divided the blacks into ten ethnic homelands, four of which are now autonomous and are called Independent States. The other six have varying degrees of self-government, and are called National States.

The majority of the homelands are poor and overpopulated. Unemployment is high, with the result that the migrant labor system has become the only source of income for many families. These areas are economically dependent on South Africa, which pays large sums of money to balance their budgets. For the residents of the homelands the greatest difficulty is the loss of mobility within South Africa. In the case of Transkei, Bophuthatswana, Venda and Ciskei, there is also the loss of South African citizenship.

Despite non-recognition of these countries by the international community, they are nevertheless a *de facto* part of the structure of South Africa.

INDEPENDENT STATES

Table 6: Religious Affiliation
South African Independent States
Census 1980 (in %)

	Transkei	Bophuthatswana	Venda	Ciskei*
Dutch Reformed Church	1.8	9.8	4.0	3.5
Anglican	10.6	6.8	0.6	5.9
Methodist	25.8	12.4	0.3	27.9
Presbyterian	5.4	0.8	0.3	7.2
Congregational	1.0	3.9	0.9	5.2
Lutheran	1.4	12.4	7.2	1.1
Apostolic	0.7	0.5	0.5	1.2
Roman Catholic	7.7	8.9	2.3	4.4
Other Christian Churches	3.4	11.1	6.4	7.5
	57.8	66.6	22.5	63.9
African Independent Churches	16.4	28.6	15.4	22.1
Total Christian	74.2	95.2	37.9	86.0
Traditional	25.8	4.8	62.1	14.0

REPUBLIC OF TRANSKEI

Transkei is situated on the southeastern coastline of South Africa. It adjoins Lesotho in the north-east. Two districts of Transkei are separated from the main area by South Africa.

Historical and Constitutional development

In the early days, the area which is now Transkei was populated by San (Bushmen) and Khoi (Hottentots). Today the majority of the population is Xhosa-speaking (95%). This area was annexed by the Cape of Good Hope and administered as a separate territory, but was later incorporated into the Union of South Africa in 1910.

When the Afrikaner National Party came to power in 1948, self-government was encouraged as part of the policy of separate development. This process commenced in 1956 and culminated in 1976 when Transkei was granted full independence from South Africa.

There have been two military coups in recent days, both conducted by Major-General Holomisa, who now heads the military government.

Socioeconomic conditions[2]

Transkei is a poor country. Although a good proportion of the land is arable and well-watered, the population density is high. It is estimated that a third of the people are landless and the average size of land holding is too small to produce enough food for a family. Thus the vast majority are dependent on wages sent home by migrant workers who currently constitute 40% of the total labor force. Income distribution tables indicate that 70% of rural homes in Transkei live below the poverty datum line. The number of children in the 0-14 age group is high (50.2%) and malnutrition is prevalent, particularly in rural areas.

People of Transkei

The official languages of Transkei are English, Xhosa and Sesotho. The Xhosa-speaking people, part of the Nguni ethnic group, consist of ten tribes. Xhosa has become the spoken language at the expense of other dialects. The other tribes include Mpondo, Mpondomise, Mfengu, Tembu and Bhaca. The Sotho

---

2   See Addendum 2 for socio-economic statistics

people are mainly situated in areas alongside Lesotho. The Griqua people, living in the north of Transkei, are of mixed descent. They had their origins in the Khoi group.

Status of Christianity

When Reverend William Shaw, a Methodist minister, arrived in 1820 with a party of British settlers, he established an English-speaking church in the neighboring area. But he had a vision to reach the indigenous people and in 1823 he took leave of his congregation and traveled northeast to establish the first mission station amongst the Xhosa people. In a few years, nine mission stations were founded, the first of which was Wesleyville. Other missions to commence pioneer work before the turn of the century were the Berlin Mission (1843), Anglicans (1855), Moravians (1863), Roman Catholics (1882), and German Baptists (1892).

In 1856 a tragedy occurred. The Xhosa people were feeling the burden of the wars with the encroaching white settlement. A Xhosa woman acted upon a vision in which she believed she was promised that the settlers would be chased from the land if all crops were destroyed and livestock killed, and that the lands and stock would be replenished. It is estimated that 25,000 people died as a result of the ensuing starvation. Mission work was extended to assist these impoverished people. Ultimately this resulted in a mass turning to Christ, and the Xhosa people became committed in their faith.

Today more than 50% of the population claim to belong to a Christian Church. Another 16% belong to an African Independent church. However, many of these people are Christian by name only and not by conviction. This can be assessed by statistics for the Methodist Church. The census report in 1980 indicates that 16.4% of the population is Methodist, but membership records of the Methodist Church account for only 6.7% of the population.

Table 7: Religious Affiliation in Transkei (Census 1980)

Protestant	39%
Traditional and no religion	26%
African Independent Churches	16%
Anglican	11%
Roman Catholic	8%

There are a number of smaller mission churches which are evangelical and there is an evangelical core in most of the ecumenical churches.

NATIONAL CHURCHES

Coordinating bodies

The Transkei Council of Churches (TCC), established in 1964, was preceded by the Transkei Missionary Conference. Today the TCC has twenty-five full members and twenty-one observer members. Many of the churches represented are from the African Independent Churches group. Ministries of the TCC include community development and a Bible-teaching ministry to the African Independent Churches through the Mennonite Central Committee.

The Evangelical Association of Transkei draws together a number of the smaller mission churches. It aims to promote evangelism and church growth and to provide fellowship for evangelical Christians.

A number of coordinating bodies exist to promote inter-church relationships between the African Independent churches. These include the African Minister's Fellowship, Amalgamation of Zionist Christian Churches and Transkei United Churches Association.

Protestant churches

Methodist Church

The Methodist Church was the first church to become established in the Transkei. Today it is still the most prominent. In 1977 the mother church, the Methodist Church of Southern Africa, was banned by the government. At that time the Methodist Church of Transkei was formed; its name was later changed to the United Methodist Church of Southern Africa. This church, with nearly 200,000 members, has now established churches in South Africa and extended its work in Transkei. In 1988 the church was unbanned and discussions are now underway with a view to reunite these two denominations.

Presbyterians

Although the Methodists were the first to establish missions in Xhosa area, the missionaries of the Glasgow Missionary Society were the first to baptize converts. In 1924, the well-known Lovedale Mission was established, becoming the first of a number of Presbyterian mission stations in Xhosa territory. An indigenous church, the Bantu Presbyterian Church, was constituted in 1923; by 1928 there were forty-four organized congregations with more than 24,000 members. Today this church is named the Reformed Presbyterian Church in Southern Africa and its members number more than 142,000 according to the 1980 census.

Dutch Reformed Church in Africa

Rietvlei, established in 1929, was the first of a number of mission stations established by the Dutch Reformed Church. Although they were late entrants to the missionary scene, they have now grown to a church of more than 12,000 members and are continuing to grow in relation to the population growth rate. Twenty-seven churches are now seeking to reach the people of Transkei. Their seminary, Decoligny Theological Seminary, is situated outside Umtata.

Twelve hospitals, situated in the rural areas, were established by the DRC in Africa but have subsequently been taken over by the government.

Anglican Church

Anglican work in Transkei began in 1855 with the establishment of St Mark's Mission among the Galeka people. As each mission station was established, schools and agricultural work were also opened. By the end of the nineteenth century, a further four mission stations had been established.

Today the work in Transkei has a separate diocese, Saint John's, with seven archdeaconries. More than 100 priests, of whom only 10% are expatriate, minister to the people. Despite the seemingly large number of clergy, there are so many remote outstations that many of them are visited only once a month by a priest. In these churches, the work of the church is being carried out by lay-people. The Anglican church is currently involved in a lay-training program to equip these people for ministry. Priests are trained at Saint Bede's Theological College outside Umtata.

Roman Catholics

Roman Catholics living in Transkei felt the need for a resident priest. Father Alexandre Baudry, a French Oblate Father, was sent to Umtata in 1882. Initially the ministry was to the colonists but it soon extended to the indigenous people. In 1887 the first mission was established and a school was opened under the care of the German sisters at Holy Cross Convent. Today the Diocese of Umtata has a church population of more than 48,000. In addition,

Catholic parishes are to be found in the diocese of Umzinkulu, Queenstown, Aliwal North and Kokstad.

The Catholic Church involves itself in social work and is responsible for children's homes and homes for the aged, schools and hostels, trade and agricultural schools. Their extensive medical work has been taken over by the state but Catholic sisters are still working at the hospitals.

African Independent Churches

The Independent Church movement began in 1884 when a black minister broke away from the Methodist Church to establish his own congregation. Since that day independent churches have mushroomed and it is estimated that there are nearly 300 of these groups, the majority of which are of the Zionist family of churches.

Some 56% of the leaders grew up in established churches. They have an average of seven and a half years' schooling[3]. Africa Inter-Mennonite Mission is working amongst these groups in a Bible-teaching ministry.

Christian activities

Evangelism

A number of the denominations of Transkei have evangelism programs which reach out to the unchurched in remote areas of the country. In addition, parachurch organizations work in specialized ministries. Scripture Union and Students' Christian Movement are reaching the youth. Hospital Christian Fellowship is active amongst medical staff. Gospel Recordings' card-talks are distributed amongst rural people. There are open opportunities to minister in the schools. Evangeli Xhosa Bible School students are taking advantage of the open doors. Youth for Christ is reaching the youth through school programs, camps and rallies.

Literature and Bible distribution

The Bible Society has an office in Umtata. In 1986 they distributed 14,579 Bibles, 263 New Testaments and 2,733 portions and selections. The first published translation was Luke's Gospel, published in 1833 by Shaw and Boyce. The present translation of the Bible dates back to 1927, but Xhosa has developed as a

---

3   Pretorius, H.L., *Sound the Trumpet of Zion*

language since those days. A new translation, the Good News in Xhosa, is underway and the New Testament has been printed.

There is a dearth of Christian literature in Xhosa, particularly in a simple form for the semi-literate.

There are bookshops in Butterworth and Idutywa. The Bible Society has a bookshop in Umtata.

Christian education

Colleges for training in Transkei include Saint Bede's Theological College (Anglican), Decoligny Seminary of the Dutch Reformed Church in Africa, and Transkei Bible College in Umtata, which is run by the Full Gospel Church of God. Evangeli Xhosa Bible School is operating in Kentani. Students working in evangelism teams reach out into the surrounding areas as part of their practical training.

Social work

In addition to churches which have social action programs, there are parachurch groups working in Transkei. These include Leprosy Mission, operating the New Life Centre. ACAT (Africa Co-operative Action Trust) operates a rural development program based on "Savings Club" schemes. In addition, they operate a training center outside Umtata. World Vision is involved in development schemes.

Needs in Transkei

Leadership training is one of the greatest needs. Many pastors are inadequately trained to cope with the growing generation of educated young people. Because of the shortage of trained pastors, the development of lay leadership is essential.

Family life has suffered due to the large number of migrant workers. Children are growing up without a father figure.

Young people are being saved through parachurch groups working among the youth. There is a danger that they withdraw from the churches they have grown up with, whereas they could act as "leaven" within these churches.

The churches have few financial resources. The people are poor and many of the men are absent due to the migrant labor system. Nevertheless the people need to recognize the need for financially supporting their pastors. A tent-making ministry might make an appropriate model.

Traditional religion still has a stronghold in many parts of Transkei, and churches, particularly in rural areas are syncretistic. Biblical teaching is needed.

BOPHUTHATSWANA

The Republic of Bophuthatswana gained its independence from South Africa in 1977, following self-governing status conferred in 1972. The name Bophuthatswana means "the place where the Tswanas live." Its leader is President Lucas M. Mangope. It consists of seven separate geographical units. The capital town is Mmabatho.

Two thirds of the population of Bophuthatswana (2.9 million) are Batswana. Other black tribes include Shangaan (91,000), North Sotho (84,000), Ndebele (62,000) and Xhosa (60,000). A further 1.2 million Batswana live in South Africa and 1.1 million in Botswana.

The economic mainstay of this country is mining, which employs some 35,000 people. The platinum mines supply 30% of the world's total production. Chrome, vanadium, asbestos and manganese are other important minerals. The economy is based on a free enterprise system.

Status of Christianity

Bophuthatswana has a long history of missionary activity. According to the 1980 census, 95% of the population claim allegiance to a Christian denomination. Church membership figures, however, do not reflect the sense of belonging which the census indicates.

Table 8: Religious Affiliation in Bophuthatswana
(1980 Census)

Protestant	50%
African Independent Churches	29%
Roman Catholics	9%
Anglican	7%
Traditional	5%

The Batswana people were among the earliest people to be evangelized. Robert Moffat of the London Missionary Society arrived in South Africa in 1817, and eventually settled in the Kuruman district. From this historic mission station he began translating the Scriptures into Setswana. The Gospel of Luke was published in 1830 and this became the first Scripture to be produced in a South African indigenous language. The first complete Bible was printed in 1857 on a hand printing press housed at Moffat's church. The work of the London Missionary Society is now part of the United Congregational Church.

According to the 1980 census, 4% of the population claim to belong to this church. At Thaba 'Nchu, over to the east of the country, the Methodists arrived in 1823 to work among a Batswana tribe. They were warmly welcomed and a church was built. Today almost half the population in this district claim to be Methodists.

African Independent Churches are increasing in number. These church groups, of which there are many, accommodate traditional values and way of life alongside biblical teaching. Their numbers increased from 25% to 28% of the total population between the years 1970 to 1980 while the percentage who adhered to traditional worship decreased from 7.8% to 5.2% of the population. The first of these indigenous churches to become established was the Native Independent Congregational Church which broke away from the London Missionary Society in 1895.

Parachurch groups

Youth for Christ has a three year program aimed at reaching every high school student over a three year period.

Life Ministry commenced its work in this country on a "tent-making" basis through their Agape movement. "Here's Life" campaigns and student work on the university campus are other areas of involvement.

VENDA

Venda is a tiny state situated in the north-east of South Africa. It is separated from the Limpopo River and Zimbabwe by a narrow strip of land. Its people, the Vhavenda, are linked ethnically to the Shona in Zimbabwe. For hundreds of years the Vhavenda people have practiced subsistence agriculture, dividing their farming plots between the new generations. Now that their farmlands have become too small to produce adequate crops, these remote people have been forced into a different way of life. Following a period of self-government, Venda accepted independence from South Africa, granted in 1979. The government is now led by President F.N. Ravela. The capital town is Thohoyandou. The official language is Luvenda.

Venda's sub-tropical climate is ideal for many cash crops such as tea, sisal, fruit and coffee. Despite the emphasis on job creation, 41% of the labor force works outside the country as migrant laborers.

Status of Christianity

Cultural religious practices are largely unchallenged. Venda is the least reached of any area in South Africa. Only 38% of the population claim to be Christian and of these, 15% belong to syncretistic African Independent Churches. However, over the past ten years, the total number of Vhavenda who claim to be Christian has increased by 6%. The African Independent Churches have grown rapidly and their percentage has increased from 11.6% to 15.4% of the total population.

Traditional religion is strongly adhered to. Lake Fundudzi is regarded as sacred and the "real" heart of Venda. Offerings are made to the spirits of the ancestors believed to live in this lake.

The largest denomination in Venda is the Evangelical Lutheran Church, who number 33,000. The work was started by missionaries of the Berlin Mission in 1872.

The first missionary to work in the area was Alexander McKidd, who initiated a Dutch Reformed work in 1863. The census indicates that nearly 12,000 people, representing 4% of the total population, belong to Dutch Reformed Churches.

CISKEI

The Republic of Ciskei is a small elongated area jutting inland from the southeastern coastline. Its population of approximately one million people is headed by President L. Sebe. In 1971 a Legislative Assembly with executive powers was established; in 1981 this former homeland became independent. A one-party state is now operating.

The official languages of Ciskei are Xhosa and English. The capital of Ciskei is Bisho. The people in this tiny state are desperately poor, with many living in areas which originated as resettlement camps. Jobs are few and the population density rate is high. Some researchers estimate this figure to be as high as 127 people per square kilometer. Significant reforms taking place include reduced taxation, a land reform program, deregulation for small businesses and incentives to industrialists. But despite these measures, two thirds of the income of the people of Ciskei is generated outside the country and the unemployment rate is excessive.

Status of Christianity

There were several early attempts to reach the Xhosa in this area. Doctor J.T. Vanderkemp of the London Missionary Society (LMS) settled among the Xhosa in 1799, but when he found little response, he decided to work among the Khoi. Another LMS missionary, Joseph Williams, arrived in 1816 and established the first mission station, but he died after eighteen months. His successor was Reverend John Brownlee, who settled at Tyumie where he established a center for evangelism and education. A prominent Xhosa Christian, who came to be regarded as a prophet, was Ntsikana.

The Glasgow Society arrived in 1823 and their missionaries established the first mission station at Tyumie as well as work among the settler community. The mission station at Lovedale later became a renowned training institute. Other early entrants to this area were the Moravians, Berlin Missionary Society, the Anglicans and the German Baptists. The missionaries considered institutional work to be part of their evangelism program. They built schools and became involved in health care.

Methodists have the largest following in this area. More than one in four claim affiliation to the Methodist denomination. The census indicates a larger following in the rural areas than in the towns, whereas the Catholics and Anglicans have stronger support in the towns.

Some 14% of the population declined to state their religion or had no religion. Of this number, 55% are urbanized. This could indicate a large number who have rejected Christianity as opposed to a strong adherence to traditional religion.

The Dutch Reformed Church was a late entrant to the area. Concerted missionary effort only commenced in 1932. A notable achievement has been the establishment of Mfesane, an organization which is involved in social welfare and training.

Other church groups represented in this area are the Assemblies of God, which, under the leadership of the late Nicholas Bhengu, made a marked impact on the Eastern Cape, the Full Gospel Church of God, Pilgrim Holiness Church, Free Methodists and Seventh Day Adventists.

The Independent Church movement, stronger in the urban areas than in the rural areas, includes followings from both the pentecostal Zionist churches and the Ethiopian groups. There do not appear to be single groups who have gained prominence, but rather a profusion of smaller groups.

Although eight out of ten people claimed allegiance to some Christian church, this large ratio is not necessarily reflected in church membership figures.

NATIONAL STATES

Table 9: Religious Affiliation
South African National States
Census 1980 (in %)

	Gazankulu	Kangwane	Kwandebele	KwaZulu	Lebowa	Qwaqwa
Dutch Reformed	1.4	1.6	5.4	0.9	4.2	26.1
Anglican	0.2	1.2	1.9	5.3	1.9	5.1
Methodist	0.3	1.8	1.8	7.2	1.9	11.4
Presbyterian	3.3			1.9	1.1	5.5
Congregational		0.8	1.8	2.3	0.2	0.4
Lutheran	0.6	1.0	2.5	5.2	7.6	0.2
Apostolic	0.6		0.2	0.2	0.4	1.4
Roman Catholic	3.8	3.5	5.6	14.0	8.2	9.6
Other Christian	10.8	12.8	6.6	3.9	2.7	7.6
	21.0	22.7	25.8	40.9	28.2	67.3
African Independent Churches	19.6	55.1	60.1	32.0	26.2	25.5
Total Christian	40.6	77.8	85.9	72.9	54.4	92.8
Traditional and Non-Christian	59.4	22.2	14.1	26.1	45.6	7.2

GAZANKULU

This small self-governing territory, consisting of three blocks, is situated in the northeastern part of South Africa. The country is governed by a legislative assembly with Professor H.W.E. Ntsanwisi as its Prime Minister. Gazankulu is home for the Tsonga people. The capital town is Giyani.

With 34% of its population working as migrants in South Africa, the majority of the population are women and children. Only 10% of this country's population are men aged twenty years and older. The high population density rate of ninety-two people per square kilometer is being exacerbated by the influx of refugees from Mozambique.

The majority of the people still cling to traditional beliefs (60%) while a further 20% belong to African Independent Churches.

The Roman Catholics are the largest single church group in the area. According to the 1980 census, some 20,000 people claim allegiance to the Catholic church. This figure possibly includes Mozambican refugees who feel a sense of affiliation to the Catholic tradition. Catholic witness in this area commenced in 1925.

The most influential church in this area is the Evangelical Presbyterian Church which grew out of the work of the Swiss Mission. Their ministry to the Tsonga people commenced in 1875. For almost fifty years it was the only church reaching this ethnic group; they played an important role in the development of the people through education, health and literature. Today they have 130 congregations with 20,000 members throughout Gazankulu (census 15,000).

Other churches represented in this area include the Dutch Reformed Church (with 3,000 members), Methodists, Anglicans, Apostolic Faith Mission and the Church of the Nazarene.

KANGWANE

Kangwane, with its population of 600,000, is the homeland of the Swazi people. The state is made up of two blocks and adjoins northern Swaziland. Siswati, the language of the Swazi people, is closely connected to Zulu. A legislative Assembly was proclaimed in 1977 with E.J. Mabuza as Chief Minister. The capital town is Louieville.

The people of Kangwane adhere firmly to traditional beliefs. One in four are purely traditional while more than 55% belong to African Independent Churches where Christianity is mingled with traditional beliefs.

The largest church in Kangwane is the Alliance Church, which grew out of the work of the Swedish Alliance Mission. It has an approximate membership of 12,000 (7% of the population). The Phumelela Bible School trains forty students a year.

Other church groups operating in this area include the Roman Catholics (3.5% of the population), Methodists (2.7%), Dutch Reformed (1.6%), and Anglican (1.3%).

Ministry to African Independent Churches is a real need.

KWANDEBELE

Kwandebele was granted self-government in 1981. Its Chief Minister is M.G. Mahlanga. The language of the people is Ndebele.

This impoverished homeland serves as a labor supply to South Africa. In 1985, 62% of Kwandebele's economically active population were migrant laborers and a further 20% were commuters. Children in the 0-14 age group comprise 53% of the resident population.

The people of Kwandebele are strong supporters of the African Independent Churches. In 1980, 60% of the population claimed affiliation to one of these churches while 14% were traditional in their beliefs. Some 5% of the people belong to the Dutch Reformed Church and a further 5% are Roman Catholics.

KWAZULU

The Zulu nation is the largest ethnic group in South Africa. The KwaZulu state, with a population of 4.4 million, is comprised of twenty-two areas, inseparably interwoven with the province of Natal. Extra-parliamentary discussions have taken place with a view to consolidating Natal and KwaZulu to form a single geographical, economic and social unit.

KwaZulu is densely populated and its people poor. A large number of children are undernourished or malnourished. There is a high degree of unemployment.

KwaZulu was granted self-government in 1977. The Paramount Chief is Goodwill Zwelethini. The Chief Minister is G. Buthelezi.

Christianity in KwaZulu

Although several earlier approaches had been made to the Zulu King for permission for missionaries to enter the region it was not until the nineteenth century that missions were established. A number of missions were involved in the evangelization of the Zulus. One of these missions was the American Board Mission whose representative visited the Zulu chief, Dingaan, in 1836. Permission was granted for them to build a school at Port Natal (now Durban). Despite drawbacks, by 1944 two schools were operating. Ten years were to elapse before they saw their first convert. The work of this mission is now incorporated into the United Congregational Church. An American Board missionary,

Newton Adams, was responsible for the first Scripture translations in 1846.

The Norwegian Missionary Society sent Reverend Hans Schroeder to work among the Zulus in 1843 but work did not commence until 1950. There was little response but Reverend Schroeder used his time to complete the first Zulu grammar. Later he published the first catechism in Zulu. Other early Lutheran groups were the Berlin Mission, Hermannsburg Mission and the Church of Sweden Mission. These missions have all combined now to form the Evangelical Lutheran Church, whose affiliation accounts for 5% of the population.

By the turn of the century, a number of missions were working amongst the Zulus. These included the Methodist Church, United Free Church of Scotland, Church of England, Church of Norway Mission, Scandinavian Independent Baptist Union, South Africa General Mission (now Africa Evangelical Fellowship), Free Methodists, Salvation Army and Roman Catholics. Today 28% of the population still adhere to traditional beliefs, while a further 25% belong to African Independent Churches. The Roman Catholics have a 14% affiliation according to the 1980 census. Methodists, Lutherans and Anglicans are other major denominations.

LEBOWA

This self-governing territory, consisting of twelve blocks of land, is situated in the north-east of South Africa. The Chief Minister is Noko Ramodike. North Sotho is the language of this country of 2.2 million people. Lebowa is composed of various tribes, the majority of which are North Sotho. Other ethno-linguistic groups include the Tsongas, Ndebeles, Tswanas and Swazis. Fifty-one percent of the population is in the 0-14 age group. The country is densely populated and the people are no longer able to derive an income from the land. This has resulted in 40% of the economically active seeking work outside the country.

One out of two people in Lebowa do not even claim to be Christian and there are pockets of people living in remote areas who have never heard the gospel. One in four belong to an African Independent Church where Christianity is blended with traditional worship. The areas with the greatest concentration of non-Christians are Sekgoses and Bolobedu.

The **Lutheran Church** is the most prominent church group in this area. Missionaries of the Berlin Mission arrived in this area in

1860. Their work soon spread across the area occupied by North Sothos. Membership totals 124,000 (Census - 7.6% of population).

The **Dutch Reformed Church** was another early entrant. Work in this area commenced in 1867 at Bethesda. Today there are twenty congregations with seventeen black and thirteen white ministers as well as fifty-seven evangelists. The church has a membership of 113,000. This church has grown from 70,649 members in 1970.

The **Roman Catholic church** has the largest number of adherents according to the census. The affiliation of 182,000 could include Mozambican refugees (Census - 14% of population).

The first **African Independent Church** in this area was the Lutheran Bapedi Church, which broke away from the Berlin Mission in 1890. These churches have grown from 13.8% of the population in 1970 to 25% of the population in 1980. This would indicate these churches are meeting real needs in the community. The growth in AIC churches has been won at the expense of those who were previously traditional worshipers. The largest of these groups is the Zion Christian Church, headquartered within Lebowa.

Needs for Lebowa

Needs for Lebowa include reaching the children and youth of the country, where 64% of the resident population is under the age of twenty; reaching the traditional people; and strengthening the AIC churches through Bible teaching.

QWAQWA

This mini-state, adjoining Lesotho, is situated in mountainous terrain. The predominant ethnic group (75%) is the Basothos. At the 1985 census the population was 181,000.

This homeland claims to be 92% Christian, but there is a high degree of nominality. For instance, the Methodist church has a membership of 2,102 in QwaQwa; yet, according to the 1980 census, more than 20,000 claim to be Methodist.

The Dutch Reformed Church is the largest church group in this area. Their membership is 41,000. This compares with 47,000 in the 1980 census. The Theological Seminary at Witsieshoek is currently training fifty-four students.

The large influx of people into this area makes it difficult to compare statistics from previous years.

BIBLIOGRAPHY

Brierley, Peter, *Church membership in South Africa*, MARC

Department of Statistics, Census Reports 1970, 1980 and 1985

Development Bank, Statistical Abstracts of Self-governing Territories in South Africa 1987

Development Bank, Statistical Abstracts SATBVC Countries 1987

Du Plessis, J., *A History of Christian Missions in South Africa*, Struik

Froise, M., *South African Christian Handbook 1986/87*, World Vision

Gerdener, G.B.A., *Recent Developments in South African Mission Field*, Marshall, Morgan and Scott

Institute for Contextual Theology, *Speaking for Ourselves*, African Independent Churches

Krige, E.J., *The Social System of the Zulus*, Shuter and Shooter

Murray, Andrew, *The Kingdom of God in South Africa*

Odendaal, J.N., *The Witness of the Church in the Ciskei*, University of Pretoria

Oosthuizen, G.C., "African Independent Churches' Centenary", in *DRC News* 7/85

Oosthuizen, G.C., et al, *Religion, Intergroup Relations and Social Change in South Africa*, Human Sciences Research Council

Pretorius, H.L., *Sound the Trumpet of Zion*, Iswen

SA Council of Churches, "Christians Debate the Validity of Violence in the Liberation Struggle", in *Ecunews*, August 1987

Serfontein, J.H.P., *Apartheid, Change and the NG Kerk*, Taurus

Smit, A.P., *God Made it Grow*, Bible Society of South Africa

South Africa 1986, Department of Foreign Affairs

Switzer, Les, "Reflections on the Mission Press in South Africa in the 19th and Early 20th Centuries", in *Journal of Theology for Southern Africa*, June 1983

Wetmore, Hugh, "Living in South Africa and Learning the Way of God", in *Transformation* Vol. 3 No 2

CHAPTER FIVE

Kingdom of Swaziland:

Balancing Christ with Tradition

KINGDOM OF SWAZILAND

Profile

Natural Features: Land area: 17,363 km^2 (6,704 sq miles). Smallest country in Southern Africa and rich in beauty.

Terrain: Divided into three geographical regions running north to south, the mountainous highveld, the populous middleveld, and the sub-tropical lowveld.

Climate: Summer rainfall ranging from 2,000 mm per annum in the highlands to 500 mm per annum in the lowveld. Temperatures vary from cool for most of the year in the highlands to very hot (40° C) and humid in the lowlands.

Population: 1986 (prov) 676,000. Annual growth rate: 3.4%. Population density: 39 per km^2, urban areas 396 per km^2.

Ethnic groups: Swazi 90%, whites 1.5% with the balance comprising Zulu, Mozambican and East African people.

Languages and Literacy: SiSwati and English are the official languages. Literacy: 65%.

Urbanization: 18%. Mbabane (population 38,000) is the capital. Manzini is the commercial center.

Government: A monarchy with 20-year-old Mswati III as Head of State. The Queen Mother has a unique role in a traditional system of dual monarchy. Legislative power is vested in an elected parliament. A cabinet with a Prime Minister is appointed by the King, assisted by the *Liqoqo*, a council of advisors.

Economy: Currency: 100 cents = 1 lilangeni (plural emalangeni). On a par with South African Rand. L1 = US$ .45 (July 1988). GDP: E423 million. GDP per capita: E660. GDP growth rate: 1981-84, 3.9%. Inflation rate: 16%. Imports: E706 million. Exports: E367 million. Agriculture as % of GDP: 23%. Main crops: sugar, timber and wood pulp.

Religion: Protestant 18%; Roman Catholic 6%; Anglicans 2%; African Independent Churches 52%; Nominal 10%; Traditional 10%; Bahai 1%; Muslim 1%.

HISTORICAL BACKGROUND

The present Swazi nation forms part of the Nguni group who migrated southward over a number of centuries. The ancestors of the Swazi people lived in Mozambique until about 1700. To escape warring Zulus they moved westward through South Africa, crossing the Lebombo mountains into what is now Swaziland.

The shrewd diplomacy of a series of successful kings welded the different clans into a nation despite onslaughts from the Zulus, the Boer farmers and British land speculators.

Swaziland gained its independence from Britain in 1968 and a Westminster type government was introduced. In 1973, however, King Sobhuza II suspended the constitution and reverted to a traditional system. At the time of his death in 1982, he had held the throne for sixty-one years.

Following King Sobhuza's death a period of instability followed. King Mswati III was crowned in 1986 at the age of eighteen and he rapidly began correcting sources of unrest and restoring the country once again to a constitutional government.

THE PEOPLES OF SWAZILAND

The Swazi people in Swaziland (closely related to the Zulu) form part of a larger grouping of Swazis, a million of whom live in South Africa and its Swazi homeland Kangwane. Swazis account for 90% of the population of Swaziland. The balance is made up of Zulus and Mozambicans, as well as an estimated 4,000 Muslims who originally came from East Africa. The small white population of approximately 10,000 is involved in commerce, trade and commercial farming.

SOCIO-ECONOMIC CONDITIONS

Swaziland has a well managed and diversified free enterprise economy. There is a modern sector which is responsible for more than 90% of the country's production and which employs about 30% of the labor force. The remainder of the people are involved in traditional agriculture or are self-employed.

Swaziland is very dependent on the South African economy. It is a member of the Customs Union (which provided 46% of its revenue in 1986/87); South African mines employ 16% of its labor force; and 84% of its imports are from South Africa.

Agriculture is the backbone of the economy. There is a marked difference between the production on private farms and the communal tenure. Swazi National Land contributes only 12% of total crop production although it covers 56% of the land. Wealth is calculated by the number of cattle owned, resulting in a very high overstocking rate.

Education in Swaziland was begun by missions and churches. Today most of the primary schools are still in the hands of churches and missions although they are assisted financially by the government. Tertiary education is provided by the University and Swaziland College of Technology. Some 7,000 school leavers enter the labor market annually; of these only 2,000 will find jobs.

Health services are operated by the government, missions and churches and private companies. The long-term aim of the government is to change the emphasis from curative to preventive health care, but progress is slow. In 1981 it was estimated that 60% of deaths were attributable to a lack of sanitation and clean water. In 1982 only 39% of the population had access to clean water.

The population growth rate of 3.4% a year is one of the highest in Africa. Increasing length of life, falling infant mortality rates and an average of 6.9 children per woman will double the population in twenty years. Some 46% of the population is in the 0-14 year age bracket. This has serious implications for the education system, for the provision of employment opportunities, and for the provision of social services such as health and welfare.

Table 1: Social Indicators in Brief

Total enrollment in education (1983)	159,271
% enrollment in primary schools	81%
% enrollment in secondary schools	17%
% enrollment in tertiary education	1.5%
Pupil/teacher ratio	29:1
Literacy rate (1976)	65%
Number of hospitals (1984)	12
Number of clinics & outreach sites	252
Population per hospital bed	294
Population per hospital & clinic	2,556
Population per doctor (1978)	7,200
Population per nurse	803
Infant mortality rate	133 per 1,000

STATUS OF CHRISTIANITY

Swaziland is a country which has been saturated with the gospel and regards itself as Christian, but it has largely rejected uncompromising Biblical faith for a form of religion which combines Christian theology and practice with traditional beliefs.

Historical review

In the mid-1830's King Sobhuza I had a vision. He saw men with skin the colour of red mealies coming with a book and round pieces of metal in their hands, and heard a voice saying "Choose the book."

Some years later, the King's son Mswati was reminded of this vision. He had heard of the teachers who had settled in what was then Basutoland and sent a messenger to ask that a teacher be sent to his country. And so, in 1844, James Allison and Richard Giddy of the Methodist Church, accompanied by two Basotho teachers, Job and Mparani, called on the Swazi leader. He received them enthusiastically and allotted them land at Mahamba. The two Basotho teachers were left behind; when Allison returned with his wife a year later, two men were ready to receive Christ and children and adults had been taught to read. The mission, however, was caught up in inter-tribal fighting, and in 1846 Allison fled across the border taking 1,000 people with him.

This retreat had an adverse affect on the history of missions. The Berlin Mission attempted to establish a work in 1860 but was refused by King Mswati. It was not until his death that new attempts were made to establish work. However, missions and churches were being established on the borders of the country. The Anglican church bought farms on the Transvaal border in the 1860's and it was from this base that Father Joel Jackson worked. For nine years he proved to the king that he was a man of peace and a trustworthy leader. In 1871 he was granted land. This became the first lasting attempt to establish work in Swaziland.

It is of significance that the first missionaries to Swaziland were Basotho evangelists. The Wesleyan's return to Swaziland was in 1880 and Daniel Msimang, a Swazi, recommenced mission work. Lutheran work in Swaziland was also started by a Swazi man who had been converted at the Berlin Mission in South Africa.

The year 1914 marked the end of the first wave of missionary endeavors and the years following saw many mission stations established across the country.

The present situation

Many denominational and mission churches are operating in Swaziland today. Furthermore, the originating missions, and more recently parachurch organizations, heavily back the existing churches. Yet the number of committed and uncompromising Christians is small and the number of church members is decreasing as a percentage of the total population. The churches held the last generation in their hands through the educational system but missed the opportunity to reach them.

The majority of church members are women. They are the backbone of the church but can never become leaders because of the women's role in the traditional structure of society. The men choose to align themselves with indigenous churches which allow them to fulfil their obligation to family traditions.

The young people are torn and confused between traditionalism and western culture. There are indications that the youth are looking for something more meaningful in life and some churches are reporting response.

Pastors are poorly trained and were ill-equipped to take over leadership when churches were handed over to nationals. The number of members per church is generally low; consequently it is difficult for churches to have full-time ministers. The result is a lack of Bible study and pastoral care. Because of the gracious qualities of respect inherent in Swazi culture, undertrained pastors tend to be intimidated both by educated, westernized people and also traditionalists. Few pastors involve themselves in the country's ethical, social or developmental affairs.

UNREACHED PEOPLES

There are pockets of **Swazis** living along ravines in remote areas who have not been reached by mainline or mission churches. One such area is along the Ngwempisi river.

Muslims number 6,000. The majority comprise expatriate Africans from Kenya, Malawi, Tanzania and Mozambique, some of whom are nationalized Swazis. A small number of Indian families account for approximately 1% of this figure. Propagation of Islam among the Swazis is slow due to the unwillingness to break with tradition. Furthermore little publicity is given to Islam in the press and no time is allocated for radio broadcasts. A mosque is situated at Ezulwini.

Baha'i communities operate in 153 localities throughout the country. There is a minimum of nine members per locality.

Traditional religion is the greatest hindrance to the spread of the gospel. Beliefs revolve around the ancestral spirits. Ancestors protect against the hazards of day-to-day living such as illness, crop failure, and deprivation. They are appealed to at times of birth, death, marriage, planting and harvesting, or any other domestic events. The ancestors of the kings are the most powerful of all spirits. Ancestors are not worshipped but rather appeased through offerings of beer and meat -- an ox is slaughtered on special occasions. The family head is responsible to address the spirits. Society is polygamous which also presents serious problems for the Christian church.

NATIONAL CHURCHES

There are three groupings of churches:

The Swaziland Conference of Churches, affiliated with the World Evangelical Fellowship and the Association of Evangelicals in Africa and Madagascar, represents eighteen churches and several parachurch groups.

The Council of Swaziland Churches is WCC-oriented and its members are the ecumenical churches.

The League of Churches was established by King Sobhuza II to discourage splintering and division.

About forty-five mission churches and mainline denominations are operating in Swaziland. The number of indigenous churches registered with the government totals thirty-one, but many groups exist who have not sought official registration. An estimated religious affiliation is listed below:

Table 2: Religious Affiliation in Swaziland

Protestants [1]	18%
Roman Catholics	6%
Anglicans	2%
African Independent Churches	52%
Baha'i & Marginal Christian	1%
Muslim	1% [2]
Traditional Religion	10% [2]
Nominal Christians	10% [2]

[1] includes an estimate for children of church-going parents
[2] estimate

Membership in the larger denominations is summarized below.

Table 3: Denominational Membership in Swaziland [1]

Roman Catholics	40,000
Church of the Province (*Anglicans*)	12,000
Assemblies of God	7,000
Church of the Nazarene	6,427
Evangelical Church	5,000
Methodist Church (*includes on-trial members*)	4,629
Lutheran Church	3,000
Seventh Day Adventists	2,639
Church of Christ (*Non-institutional*)	2,600
Free Evangelical Assemblies	2,000
Africa Evangelical Church	2,000
Alliance Church	1,000
Libandla Levangeli Lenkhululeko	1,000
African Methodist Episcopal	850
Church Emmanuel Wesleyan Church	700
Rhema Churches	650
Apostolic Faith Mission	600

[1] Few churches keep accurate records and many of the above figures are estimates given by churches.

Roman Catholics

The first Catholic missionaries to Swaziland were the Reverend Fathers Joachim Rosetto and Peregrine Bellezi who arrived in Swaziland from Italy in 1913. They were from the Order of Mary's Servants. Working from Mbabane and St Joseph's mission near Manzini, they established churches and schools. By 1926 there were seven schools with a total of 1,272 students and a Catholic population of 4,345. The work grew rapidly and by 1963 ten mission stations and sixty outstations were established.

The first four sisters to enter Swaziland were from Mantellate Servants of Mary in Italy. They arrived in 1922 and by 1935 had established a novitiate house. By 1963 there were sixty professed sisters working in eight convents under the order African Sisters of the Servants of Mary.

The first Swazi to be ordained was Reverend Father Albert Mndebela in 1954. The first Swazi bishop, Right Reverend Bishop Zwane, was ordained in 1976.

The Swaziland Mission was separated from the Natal Vicariate in 1923 and the Prefecture Apostolic of Swaziland was constituted. In 1939 it was elevated to the rank of Vicariate Apostolic and in 1951 became the Diocese of Bremersdorp (town later changed to Manzini). Right Reverend Manager L.M. Ndlovu is the Apostolic Administrator. Today the Church has a Catholic population of 40,000. Thirty-five priests, of whom ten are Swazis, minister at twenty churches and chapels and nearly one hundred preaching points. There are seven brothers and one hundred sisters serving in fifteen convents. Forty-five primary schools and ten high schools fall under their care, as well as a hospital and seven clinics.

Anglican Church

In 1871 the King offered the Anglicans land near to his royal kraal to build a mission and educational institution, and so the Usuthu Mission was established. Father Joel Jackson spent twenty years developing the work and setting up schools and clinics.

Until 1950 the church was part of the Diocese of Zululand, after which it became known as the Diocese of Zululand and Swaziland. At independence in 1968, a new Diocese of Swaziland was formed which became a turning point for growth. Three more parishes were opened, local clergy began assuming greater responsibility in the life of the church, and in 1975 Bernard Mkhabela was consecrated as the first Swazi bishop. The church has a vision for growth and churches are being planted in newly developed areas. In the period between 1968 to 1978, thirteen new churches were planted.

Thokoza Community Centre is situated at Mbabane. Besides being an educational center, it has become a place of fellowship for church members.

It is estimated that there are 12,000 members, the majority of whom are women. There are twenty-three clergy, and of this number only three are expatriates.

Protestant Churches

African Evangelical Church (AEC)

In 1890, the South African General Mission (now Africa Evangelical Fellowhip) sent Reverend J. Baillie to start a mission in Swaziland. Work was commenced at Bethany Mission from whence it gradually moved southward as new mission stations were established. The church became autonomous in 1962 and is now known as Africa Evangelical Church. Expatriate missionaries working in Swaziland serve under the national church. Today there are forty-one churches and preaching points cared for by ten AEC workers. The church is responsible for one high school and two secondary schools.

Scandinavian Churches

The first of the Scandinavian missions to arrive in Swaziland was the Scandinavian Alliance Mission in 1892 (later changed to The Evangelical Alliance Mission when its head-quarters moved to the USA). Work commenced at Bulunga on the Usuthu River, but they later moved to a higher altitude to avoid malaria. The majority of the churches, which now number fifty-six, are situated in the south of the country. In 1974 these churches became independent and are now known as the Evangelical Church. A Bible School operates at Ezulwini. The Evangelical Bible Church, an English-speaking church for the 'colored' community, have two congregations.

Early in the history of the mission a number of breakaways occurred:

Swedish Alliance Mission was formed in 1913. The church which grew out of this work is called the Alliance Church of Swaziland.

A split from the Alliance Church resulted in the formation of the *Swedish Free Church* now under national leadership.

A split from the Norwegian Evangelical Church (now Libandla Levangeli Lenkululeko) resulted in the formation of *Free Gospel Mission*.

The work of the Swedish Holiness Union Mission has resulted in the establishment of the *Holiness Union Church*.

Church of the Nazarene

Work started in the north in 1910 when Reverend Harmon Schmelzenbach arrived in Swaziland. Soon after the missionaries arrived they felt the need to become involved in a caring ministry and today the church is deeply involved in education and medical work. The first school was opened in 1911. Evangelism is an important part of Nazarene education. Ten percent of Swaziland's pupils are in Nazarene schools.

Professional medical work was started at Pigg's Peak in 1921 but was moved to Manzini in 1925 where a modern 300 bed hospital with a nurses' training college now operates.

The Swaziland Nazarene Bible College is situated at Siteki and trains pastors for Swaziland and further afield.

The church is organized into four districts with a total of ninety-three churches. The total of 6,427 members includes full and probationary members. Sunday School enrollment totals 19,251. The newer Southern district is recording excellent growth with tent campaigns being the major means of evangelism.

Methodists

After the abortive attempt to plant a mission in 1846, Reverend Allison settled the 1,000 fugitives from inter-tribal war at Indaleni in Natal. Among the refugee Swazis was a young lad, Daniel Msimang, who grew to manhood and was ordained as a Methodist minister. Msimang decided to revive the Swaziland Mission which he had fled thirty-five years earlier, and despite hardships and threats to his life, he established a stable work. By the time missionaries arrived ten years later, there were three circuits in Swaziland with 300 full members. In 1954 there were 2,280 full members, but the last thirty years show little growth since the full membership only totalled 2,514 in 1985.

Pentecostal Churches

Assemblies of God is the largest of the Pentecostal churches. Nicholas Benghu conducted tent campaigns in the early 1960s, and as a result churches were planted, mainly in the south. The churches grew rapidly until today there are an estimated 7,000 members.

Other pentecostal groups include Full Gospel Church of God, United Pentecostal Church of Swaziland and the Apostolic Faith Mission.

Rhema Bible Church was a newcomer to the scene. A public criticism of the "Feast of the First Fruits" recently caused a severe reaction and resulted in the first Christian missionary to be detained, tried and declared a prohibited immigrant. This action resulted in the withdrawal of the Rhema churches from Swaziland.

African Independent Churches

These churches have a far greater appeal to Swazis than mission churches do, since they blend Christianity with traditional forms of worship. Approximately 55% of those who claim to be Christian belong to these syncretistic churches. It is easy for them to move freely between mission and independent churches because of the universalistic view they commonly hold.

There are two groupings of Independent Churches:

The faster-growing groups are charismatic *Zionists* who seek to combine Christian teaching with ancestral veneration. The degree of syncretism varies from church to church.

The *Ethiopian* groups, many of whom are breakaways from mainline denominations, draw heavily on Old Testament patterns of worship mingled with traditional forms. The United Christian Church is an Independent Church which has a sounder theological base.

Thirty-one of these Independent Churches currently have official registration, but there are many more groups who have not registered. It is estimated that a total of sixty to seventy of these groups exist, many of whom are very small.

Some of the larger groups include:

- Apostolic Holy Catholic Church in Zion
- Christian Catholic Church in Zion of South Africa
- Christian Catholic Holy Spirit Church in Zion
- Independent Methodist Church
- Saint John's Apostolic Faith Church
- Swazi Christian Church in Zion of South Africa
- Zion Christian Church

The Mennonites are involved in a Bible teaching ministry among the Independent Churches.

FOREIGN MISSIONS

Between thirty and forty missionary societies and parachurch organizations are operating in Swaziland, including a Nigerian missionary society "Deeper Christian Life Ministry." There are approximately 280 expatriate missionaries and Christian workers, a large number of whom are involved in institutional and development work. This gives an average of 350 members per expatriate church worker.[1]

At a time when national local churches should be reaching out to win Swaziland for Christ, expatriates are entering the country to

---

1   This figure includes the Roman Catholic Church and Trans World Radio whose workers are not directly involved in ministry in Swaziland

become involved in evangelism. The question is whether the church is ready or willing to accept this role. Paternalistic attitudes of the past have resulted in weak leadership. Lack of finances prevent the church from becoming involved in extensive outreach programs.

CHRISTIAN ACTIVITIES

Evangelism

The churches of Swaziland need a spiritual awakening. Many pastors lack vision and commitment. A number of churches do however have evangelistic programs which are proving to be effective. The Church of the Nazarene is using tent missions as a means of planting new churches. The Back to God Crusade, a ministry of the Assemblies of God, is reaching out into urban and rural areas and many are turning to God.

Mass evangelism crusades have been conducted by New Life for All and Christ for All Nations. Africa Enterprise, in cooperation with local churches, conducted a mission in 1988.

Parachurch agencies are involved in outreach programs. Scripture Union has an effective ministry among school children and students. Students' Christian Movement operates at a tertiary level along with Catholic and Anglican societies. Organizations such as Campus Crusade, Mbabane Church Youth Centre, ACAT and Hospital Christian Fellowship have evangelism as their primary goal.

Broadcasting

Swaziland Broadcasting Corporation offers free time for religious broadcasts on the national network. Swaziland Conference of Churches is responsible for production of these programs with the cooperation of twenty-six denominations. Sixty programs are transmitted each week in English and SiSwati

Trans World Radio has a powerful radio station in Manzini, but by agreement its target audiences are outside of Swaziland. However, recordings in Zulu are readily picked up and appreciated. Responses reveal a hunger for the Word of God.

Religious programs from South African radio stations are also received.

Several religious programs are shown over Swazi Television, the majority of which are produced externally.

Literature

The early missionaries who came to Swaziland chose to learn Zulu rather than the language of the people, Siswati, and as they developed the education system, they used the Zulu medium for education. A literature ministry began to develop when the Nazarene Mission installed a hand operated printing press at Siteki in 1925 which was later moved to Manzini. Local papers, hymnals, catechisms and other material were produced, all in Zulu. The choice of Zulu as a medium of instruction presented difficulties which resulted in Zulu becoming the language of the educated, while the non-educated, who were unable to fully understand Zulu were isolated.

Since independence in 1968, Siswati has been developed as a written language. Education in Siswati developed incrementally, and today, 31% of the population has received an education in Siswati. The church is once again faced with a problem since the amount of Christian literature available in Siswati is very limited. The cost of producing literature for this small population group is one of the factors involved.

There are currently no publishers of Christian literature in Swaziland. There are two Christian bookshops in Manzini, the largest of which is the Nazarene bookshop, and there are two small bookshops in Mbabane.

The production of Christian literature in Siswati is vital if the generation of the future is to be won for Christ.

Christian education

The first formal attempt to establish Christian education was in 1913 when the Nazarene Mission began a Bible School at Endzingeni. They later moved this work to Siteki. They are currently training seventy-eight students, the majority of whom are Swazi, but a number from neighbouring states are also undergoing training.

Other Protestant colleges operating in Swaziland include:

- Emafini Training Centre (Life Ministries) at Mbabane
- Emmanuel Wesleyan Church at Joy
- Mission Manzini Bible School (Church of Christ)
- New Haven Bible Institute (Free Evangelical Assemblies)
- Swaziland Bible Training Centre

- Swaziland Evangelical Bible Institute - operated by Evangelical Church, TEAM and Africa Evangelical Church
- United Pentecostal College

The Assemblies of God International will soon be opening a college in the Ezulwini Valley. A number of missions offer correspondence courses, including the Baptist Mission who offer "Bibleway" courses.

Theological Education by Extension programs are operated by the Mennonites as well as a number of the Bible Colleges. The Catholics have a minor seminary in Manzini. The University has a Department of Theological and Religious studies. The Conference of Churches has formed a Theological Commission to establish closer links between the colleges.

Bible translation and needs

It is only recently that translation of the Scriptures was commenced in SiSwati, prior to which the Zulu Bible was used. In 1976 the first Scripture ever to be published in Siswati, the Gospel of Mark, was presented to the late King Sobhuza II. The first complete New Testament was published in 1981. Psalms was published in 1986. The Bible Society report a total of 4,086 New Testaments, 3,952 portions and 395 sections of Scripture distributed in 1986 in SiSwati. In addition, a total of 14,932 Bibles were distributed in English, Zulu or other languages.

Social concerns

Missions and churches have been involved in institutional work for many years. Of the Protestant churches, the Church of the Nazarene has been a leader in this field; in the early days, schools were taught by missionaries and pastors in the church. The first such school was started in 1911. Today there are thirty-nine Nazarene schools with 400 teachers and 12,000 students. In addition a teacher training college in Manzini graduates fifty new teachers each year. Many of the other churches are working in the field of education. The government is now participating in mission and church schools through the financing of teachers, but administration of schools remains under the care of missions and churches. The Catholics also have deep roots in the education system with fifty-five schools under their care.

The medical aspect of missionary work was included at all Nazarene mission stations with simple medical care provided by missionaries. The first nurse arrived in 1916 and by 1920 clinics were operating at Pigg's Peak, Endzingeni and Siteki. The Raleigh Fitkin Hospital was opened in 1927, and is now a modern 300-bed training hospital for Registered Nurses and Midwives. Good Shepherd Hospital at Siteki, run by the Catholics, serves the eastern ridge of Swaziland. Campus Crusade, Seventh Day Adventists, Holiness Union Church, Free Evangelical Church, Alliance Church, Emmanual Wesleyan Church and ACAT also serve in the medical field. Medical care is provided for lepers at Thembelihle, a ministry of the Church of the Nazarene, in cooperation with the Leprosy Mission and Department of Health.

A number of agencies assist in development and training schemes throughout the country. These include Council of Swaziland Churches, Caritas, Lutheran World Federation, Mennonite Central Committee, Bread for the World, ACAT, World Vision, Tear Fund and the Conference of Churches.

The number of refugees from Mozambique is uncertain, but is estimated to be in the region of 12,000. A number of agencies are involved in assistance to these Mozambicans. A large influx of Swazis from South Africa has settled in the Ndzevane area. Political refugees from South Africa have also found asylum in Swaziland.

NEEDS IN SWAZILAND

A spiritual awakening is needed in Swaziland. Pastors need a new vision of unsaved people around them and a commitment to reach them. Further training is needed for pastors through formal training and pastors' conferences.

Ministry to men is necessary. Existing programs of the church do not appear to be effective in reaching men. Many national pastors feel the only way to reach men is through personal evangelism.

Continued youth evangelism can be the means of building a strong church for the future. Many church leaders and laymen were won to Christ as young people, and today ministry to the youth is producing encouraging results.

Expatriate missionaries are required to assist in strengthening leadership and in institutional work. However, they need to come humbly, to accept a partnership role, and to respect a culture they don't understand.

There are few full-time pastors. The ratio of pastors to church members is very low -- on average, fifty members per congregation in Protestant churches. Evangelism and church growth programs aimed at increasing membership could enable these congregations to employ their pastors full-time. More emphasis is required on encouraging responsibility towards supporting churches and pastors.

Christians willing to take up lectureships at the University could have a 'tentmaking' ministry.

Increased involvement of pastors in social affairs could affect the future directions of the Christian gospel in Swaziland.

BIBLIOGRAPHY

Africa Research Bulletin (Political & Economic Series)

Africa South of the Sahara, Europa Publications, 1986

Annual Statistical Bulletin, 1984, Central Statistical Office

Barrett, David, *World Christian Encyclopedia*

Booth, Alan R., *Swaziland: Tradition and Change in a Southern African Kingdom*, Westview

Church Co-operation in Swaziland: A Test for Western Church Presence in Africa, Berlin Mission (Author unknown)

Economic Review and Outlook, Prime Minister's Office, Jan 1987

Fair, T.J.D., *Rural-Urban Balance*, Africa Institute

50 Years of Missionary Work 1914-1964

4th National Development Plan 1983/84 - 1987/88, Government of the Kingdom of Swaziland

Herbst, D.A.S., *Pragmatic Swaziland Returns to Normality*, South Africa Forum

Johnson, Dave, *Guide to Botswana, Lesotho & Swaziland*, Winchester Press

Key Results of the Swaziland National Nutrition Status, Survey by the National Nutritional Council

Kusel, Gerhard, *Church Co-operation in Swaziland*

Malan, J.S., *Swazi Culture*, Africa Institute

Matsebula, J.S.M., *The Church of the Province in Swaziland*

Mears, Gordon, *Methodism in Swaziland*, Methodist Missionary Department

Perkins, Floyd J., *A History of Christian Missions in Swaziland*

Provisional Census Figures, 1986, Department of Statistics

Swaziland Conference of Churches, *Annual Report 1986/87*

Walts, C.C., *Dawn in Swaziland*, Society for the Propagation of the Gospel in Foreign Parts, 1922

Addendum 1
Statistical Review of the Countries of Southern Africa

	Botswana	Lesotho	Namibia	South Africa [1]	Swaziland
Natural Features					
Area (km^2)	582,000	30,355	842,269	1,121,944	17,363
Arable land (%)	5	9	1	13	14.5
Annual rainfall (mm p.a.)	250-650	503-1,308	100-400	60-1,000	500-2,000
Population					
De facto population	1,131,700	1,577,000	1,180,000	27,722,300	676,000
Density per km^2	1.6	51	1.4	24.7	39
Urbanized (%)	21	16	26	56	18
0-14 age group (%)	48.0	41	42	35	45
Economy [2]					
GDP (US $million)	1,914	307	971	49,549	190
GDP per capita (US$)	998	195	823	1,266	297
GNP per capita (US$) [3]	-	584	-	1,368	-
Agriculture as % of GDP	7	20	6	6	23
Mining as % of GDP	4.8	16	47.7	21	6.8
% of economically active employed in agriculture	7.6	56	50	14	36 [4]
Migrants as % of labor force	18	60	-	-	18
Education					
Total enrollment	254,554	287,468	350,080	6,602,646	159,271
% in primary schools	87	90	77	64	81
% in secondary schools	12	9	21	30	17
% in tertiary education	5	1	1	5	1.5
Pupil/teacher ratio	30:1	48:1	32:1	32:1	29:1
Literacy rate (%)	35	65	35	64	65
Health					
Number of hospitals	14	20	62	701	12
Number of clinics & health centers	348	93	158	1,563	252
Population per hospital bed	463	607	130	193	294
Populaton per clinic & health center	2,692	13,955	7,493	13,758	2,556
Population per doctor	6,000	12,265	4,289	476	7,200
Population per nurse	602	3,090	302	654	803
Infant mortality rate (per 1,000)	79	94	100	55	133

[1] Statistics include SA National States but exclude Independent States

[2] US exchange rate calculated on July 1988 exchange rates

[3] Migrant wages added in where applicable

[4] Includes formal and non-formal

Addendum 2
Statistical Review of Independent States
within Southern Africa (TBVC 1985 Statistics)

	Transkei	Bophuth-atswana	Venda	Ciskei
Natural Features				
Area (km^2)	43,653	44,000	7,760	9,000
Arable land (%)	26	6.5	11	13
Annual rainfall (mm per year)	900	500	900	650
Population				
De facto population	2,933,206	1,740,600	459,819	750,000
Density per km^2	67	40	64	97
Urbanized (%)	5	15	3	35
0-14 age group (%) [1]	50	36	43	41
Economy [2]				
GDP - US$ million	656,215	543,058	110,295	178,584
GDP - R million	1,458,250	1,206,796	245,100	396,854
GDP per capita - US$	205	311	239	238
GDP per capita - R	457	693	532	529
GNP per capita - US$ [3]	403	538	397	458
GNP per capita - R	896	196	884	1019
Agric. as a % of GDP (market)	5.3	0.2	5	0.8
Mining as a % of GDP	0.1	36	3	-
% of economy actively employed in agriculture	18.2	4.6	19.2	10
Migrants as a % of labor force	40	37	41	29
Education				
Total enrollment	870,213	526,274	186,232	253,698
% in primary schools	74	67	72	77
% in secondary schools	24	31	24	21
% in tertiary education	1.2	1.3	2.6	1.4
Pupil/teacher ratio	45:1	38:1	32:1	40:1
Literacy rate	53%	80%		
Health				
Number of hospitals	32	11	4	7
# of clinics & health centers	219	162	73	95
Population per hospital bed	319	374	346	247.5
Population per clinic & health center	13,455	11,229	9,200	7,978
Population per doctor	11,827	16,420	24,210	3,989
Population per nurse	536	651	603	223

[1] Includes migrant workers
[2] US$ exchange rate calculated on July 1988 rates
[3] Includes wages earned outside the country

Addendum 3
Statistical Review National States within Southern Africa
(1985 Statistics)

	Gazankulu	Kangwane	Kwandebele	Kwazulu	Lebowa	Qwaqwa
Natural Features						
Area (km^2)	6,565	3,823	3,244	36,074	22,000	655
Arable land (%)	14.8	29	15	20	14.8	16.4
Rainfall (mm per year)	800	800	-	900	500	800
Population						
De facto						
population (1985)	607,461	464,481	296,864	4,462,498	2,222,000	225,672
Density per km^2	93	122	92	124	102	345
Urbanized (%)	4	14	9	23	6	12
0-14 age group (%) [1]	49	47	43	44	48	41
Economy [2]						
GDP US $ million	118,404	52,200	37,467	548,626	265,504	51,435
GDP R million	263,120	115,990	83,260	1,219,170	590,010	114,300
GDP per capita US$	195	130	126	122	119	228
GDP per capita R	388	249	280	273	265	507
GNP per capita US$ [3]	377	421	538	395	306	666
GNP per capita R	838	937	1,196	878	681	1,481
Agriculture as a						
% of GDP	20	12	9	61	5	4
Mining as % of GDP	1.7	6	-	2	7	-
% of economically active employed in agriculture	14	13	3.7	11	16	3
Migrants as a % of labor force	34	42	62	5	40	25
Education						
Total enrollment	240,548	155,038	152,990	1,237,759	723,017	96,684
% in primary schools	78	79	79	80	72	67
% in secondary schools	19	20	20	19.5	26	29
% in tertiary education	1.5	1.0	1.0	0.5	1.1	3.3
Pupil/teacher ratio	40:1	40:1	41:1	49:1	43:1	34:1
Health						
Number of hospitals	6	3	1	30	4	2
Number of clinics & health centers	100	103	29	171	132	18
Population per hospital bed	345	495	581	490	485	1,070
Population per clinic & health center	6,457	4,649	10,554	7,746	17,357	13,327
Population per doctor	7,508	16,513	51,011	15,845	60,292	17,134
Population per nurse	453	729	1,314	772	589	764

[1] Migrant laborers added to this figure
[2] Calculated at July 1988 exchange rate
[3] Includes wages earned outside the country

Addendum 4
South African Religious Affiliation [1]
According to Census Reports

Race	Church Group	1960	1970	1980
		--------(in thousands)--------		
White	Reformed	1,615	1,847	2,085
	Pentecostal	138	219	408
	Anglican	384	404	461
	Lutheran	34	42	43
	Other Protestants	554	718	823
	Roman Catholic	192	309	388
	TOTAL	2,917	3,540	4,208
Colored	Reformed	450	590	684
	Pentecostal	97	172	329
	Anglican	261	332	360
	Lutheran	73	95	102
	Other Protestants	371	485	499
	Roman Catholic	119	197	266
	TOTAL	1,371	1,871	2,441
Asian	Reformed	-	-	3.4
	Pentecostal	6.5	11	36.5
	Anglican	6	7.2	7.6
	Lutheran	-	-	0.7
	Other Protestants	5	19.8	33
	Roman Catholic	10	15	20
	TOTAL	27.5	53	101.2
Black	Reformed	563	1,069	1,372
	Pentecostal	355	736	992
	Anglican	752	982	1,165
	Lutheran	542	812	940
	Other Protestants	2,135	5,617	9,107
	Roman Catholic	755	1,375	1,996
	AIC	2,313	2,716	5,127
	TOTAL	7,415	13,307	20,699
All Races	Reformed	2,628	3,506	4,144
	Pentecostal	596	1,138	1,766
	Anglican	1,403	1,725	1,993
	Lutheran	649	949	1,085
	Other Protestants	3,065	6,840	10,462
	Roman Catholic	1,076	1,896	2,670
	AIC	2,313	2,716	5,127
	GRAND TOTAL	11,731	18,771	27,250

[1] Includes Transkei, Bophuthatswana, Venda, and Ciskei

Regional Religious Statistics in %

	Botswana	Lesotho	Namibia*	South Africa* [1]	Swaziland [1]	TBV [2]	TOTAL
Protestant	17	15	65	41.5	18	40.9	36
Methodist	0.2	0.2	0.2	8.9	0.6	20.1	8.8
DRC	0.4	0.3	4.7	13.9	0.1	4.5	9.8
Congregational	1.8	-	0.3	1.9	-	2.3	1.7
Lutheran	1.9	-	44.5	3.5	0.4	5.0	4.5
SDA	0.6	0.2	1.6	0.1	0.4	-	0.13
Presbyterian	-	-	-	2.1	-	3.6	-
Roman Catholics	2.6	49	16	9.6	6	7.8	10.7
Anglicans	1	5	7	6	2	8.7	5.8
AIC	30	9	6	21	52	20.3	27.4
Traditional	38.4	7	6	15	10	22.1	16.8
Nominal/no religion	10	15	-	2.5	10	-	2.5
Muslim	0.2	1	-	1.4	1	-	0.9
Baha'i	0.8	0.2	-	-	1	-	-
Hindu	-	-	-	2.1	-	-	-

* 1980 Census

[1] Includes Ciskei

[2] Transkei, Bophuthatswana and Venda